Introduction

About This Book

Most Americans take pride in the constitution that established our system of self-government. But in 1787 the men—called Framers—who crafted it at the Constitutional Convention weren't at all certain about the decisions they were making. They debated heatedly, each predicting the frightful results of the others' ideas. Then they negotiated, hoping that their compromises would head off disaster and provide stable ways to govern their new country.

In some cases, though, the structures of our government—the parts that the Framers hardwired into the Constitution—can cause havoc in real life. Some of the crises we've faced since 1787 have resulted from—or were helped along by—limitations, ambiguities, and flatly bad ideas in the Constitution.

It might be appealing to believe that, because the Constitution and our country have survived this long, they'll always do so. But the Framers were not so confident. Perhaps you shouldn't be, either.

What Is a Constitution? Why Have One?

A constitution is an agreement that describes how an organization is governed. It is different from a collection of laws. The purpose of a constitution is to determine who *makes* the laws, how those decision makers are chosen, how long they serve, and what powers they have.

Constitutions can be broad outlines or detailed rules about how to make laws. They can emerge through discussion or by force.

Almost all countries, except Britain, New Zealand, and Israel, have written constitutions. So do all fifty states, Puerto Rico, most American Indian Nations, and many organizations, including civic groups, clubs, and schools.

Regardless of how it is developed and what it contains, a constitution is intended to help a group of people accept leadership and reduce friction. That's the idea, at any rate.

From Independence to a Constitutional Convention

In the Declaration of Independence, issued on July 4, 1776, "the thirteen united States of America" pronounced themselves

"Free and Independent States…
[with] full Power to levy War, conclude
Peace, contract Alliances, establish
Commerce, and to do all other Acts
and Things which Independent States
may of right do."
—The Declaration of Independence

But their independence was about the only thing these states could agree on. Did you notice that "united" isn't capitalized in "united States" in some versions of the Declaration? The term was merely a vague and not very accurate description.

The states were Free and Independent not only from Britain but also from each other. Thirteen disjointed minirepublics were strung along the Atlantic seaboard, not really part of a cohesive country under a single government. Each state had its own political system, money, and in many cases, a newly drafted constitution.

The people living in these states did not generally think of themselves as Americans.

❧ ❦

"Virginia, Sir, is my country."

—Thomas Jefferson

"Massachusetts is our country."

—John Adams

❧ ❦

Without a king to order them around, the states had to figure out how to get along with each other and how to reach decisions everyone would abide by, even when some states objected to them.

❧ ❦

"It is the first instance, from the creation of the world…that free inhabitants have been seen deliberating on a form of government."

—James Madison

❧ ❦

Each state sent delegates to a sort of governing body, the Confederation Congress. There, all together in one room, they tried to resolve such disputes as borderlines, especially on the endless-seeming western frontier, and how much money to cough up to pay for the war they were fighting.

The separate states operated under a set of rules or treaties called the Articles of Confederation and Perpetual Union. These had been devised in 1777 to carry out the war, though they didn't go into effect until 1781. The Articles set up a "league of friendship," as the states described their alliance.

Severe problems surfaced almost immediately. Every state was allotted one vote in this Congress, regardless of its size. But big states with large populations, such as Virginia, argued that they were entitled to more votes than little ones, such as Rhode Island. Furthermore, the delegates often didn't show up and, when they did, they spent much of their time bickering, after which they went home empty-handed and frustrated.

There was a limit to what the delegates could accomplish. The Articles had given Congress few powers beyond making treaties with other countries and printing money, which turned out

AMERICA'S FIRST PRESIDENT

The Articles of Confederation established the office of the presidency, with each appointed executive serving one year. So America's first president was not George Washington but John Hanson, a public official and revolutionary from Maryland. As explained at the One and Only Presidential Museum in Williamsfield, Ohio, Washington was our ninth! However, not one of the first eight presidents had any real power.

to be nearly worthless. Probably worst of all, the national government was not allowed to tax the citizenry. All it could do was issue requests, called requisitions, for money from the states, which often ignored them. Consequently, the treasury didn't have enough money even to pay the soldiers who had fought—and won—the Revolutionary War.

In June 1783, four hundred of those soldiers stormed Congress's headquarters in Philadelphia, clamoring for their back pay, and locked the delegates inside. When the officials were finally released, they had to run for their lives. They stayed a step ahead of the soldiers, conducting business in a series of temporary quarters in Maryland, New Jersey, and New York.

In 1786, Congress tried to requisition $3.8 million—worth about $100 million today—to pay off war debts, including soldiers' back pay. The states forked over a measly $663. It wasn't long before Alexander Hamilton and others referred to the "imbecility" of the Articles of Confederation.

Meanwhile, states imposed their own taxes on residents, which had to be paid in gold. Many farmers lost their land and were thrown into paupers' prisons. In Massachusetts, a band of two thousand men rebelled. Armed with pitchforks and led by Daniel Shays, a former captain of the Continental Army, they executed hit-and-run vigilante raids on munitions depots, surrounded courthouses, and mobbed sheriffs to protest their rising debts.

Both the national government and the states were in turmoil. Neither the

Articles of Confederation nor the states' own constitutions provided a solution.

George Washington despaired. "I predict the worst consequences from a half-starved, limping government, always moving upon crutches and tottering at every step," he lamented.

His friend General Henry Lee begged Washington to use his influence to quell the uprising. Realizing that the crises went far beyond rampaging farmers, Washington responded, "Influence is not government. Let us have one by which our lives, liberties, and properties will be secured."

Monumental change was needed, and quickly, if the "united States" was to survive as a genuine union. A likely alternative might be dissolving into several separate, sparring countries. To prevent such chaos, Congress called for a convention of delegates from the states to convene in Philadelphia on May 13, 1787.

Distinguished Characters

At first, hardly anyone showed up. Many dreaded abandoning their families, farms, and businesses to make the tiresome, jarring trek by stagecoach or horseback. The city had never seen as much rain as it did that spring, and the roads were clogged with mud.

But by May 25, enough people had gathered in the Assembly Room at the State House to begin deliberations. Selected by their state legislatures, the delegates came from large states, small ones, slave-owning and free.

Most were prominent men of means—yes, all fifty-five delegates who attended at various times were men—lawyers, doctors, or merchants. Many were young. Twenty-six-year-old Jonathan Dayton of New Jersey, who had fought in the Revolutionary War when he was only sixteen, was the youngest. James Madison of Virginia, later described as the "father" of the Constitution, was thirty-four. Hamilton was also in his early thirties.

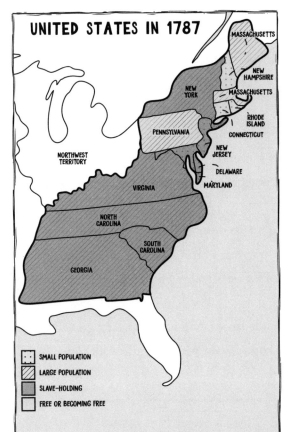

UNITED STATES IN 1787

- SMALL POPULATION
- LARGE POPULATION
- SLAVE-HOLDING
- FREE OR BECOMING FREE

States called themselves large either because they had a large population or because, like Georgia and South Carolina, they hoped to grow quickly. Pennsylvania, Connecticut, and Rhode Island were ending slavery but owners there still held people enslaved. Rhode Island did not send anyone to the Constitutional Convention. Vermont considered itself an independent country but none of the other states recognized it as one.

The oldest delegate—eighty-one-year-old author, statesman, inventor, and diplomat Benjamin Franklin—arrived in a sedan chair carried by prisoners.

Yet no one was more important than Washington, who had led the successful revolt against British rule. Admirers gathered outside the State House to greet him with applause and cheers. The delegates elected him President of the Constitutional Convention. He sat quietly at the front of the room in a wooden chair.

Thomas Jefferson, then the American ambassador to France, later called these leaders "an assembly of demi-gods."

Congress had instructed the delegates to revise the Articles of Confederation, but they knew that much more than mere revision was needed. Working six days a week for just under four months, at tables for two fitted out with quill pens and candlesticks, in a stifling room behind barred doors and latched windows, they concocted an entirely new and daring kind of government, faults and all.

IF IT WAS SECRET, HOW DO WE KNOW WHAT HAPPENED?

One of the first decisions the Framers made was to keep their proceedings secret. That way, they could speak—and change—their minds without worrying about being embarrassed in public.

As a matter of personal honor, they kept their promise even when they vehemently disagreed with each other. The Convention's secretary, William Jackson, destroyed drafts of the delegates' work, keeping only an account of proposed resolutions and the tally of votes.

James Madison sat in the front row and took detailed notes on the debates, though these were not published until 1840, four years after his death. Scholars now know that, over the years, he edited his notes for political purposes, so they are not completely accurate.

Several other Framers also occasionally made notes. We have a pretty good idea of the general arguments presented in Philadelphia, but we don't always know who made them or exactly what the delegates said.

Preamble

❧ ❧

"We the People of the United States, in Order to form a more perfect Union, establish Justice, insure domestic Tranquility, provide for the common defense, promote the general Welfare, and secure the Blessings of Liberty to ourselves and our Posterity, do ordain and establish this Constitution for the United States of America."

❧ ❧

This statement opens the United States Constitution. It's called the Preamble because it "walks before" the rest of the document. Even though it's the first paragraph, composing it was one of the last tasks the Framers took up before signing their Constitution and going home.

Actually one Framer in particular did the job—Gouverneur Morris. A delegate from Pennsylvania, Morris spoke up more often than anyone else.

Morris didn't create the Preamble from scratch. He borrowed ideas from the constitutions of several states, including Massachusetts and Pennsylvania. Other Framers had also drafted a previous version of a preamble a month earlier.

Morris seems to have had two basic reasons for editing the first preamble. One was to bring the country's widely dispersed citizenry together under the canopy of the new Constitution. The other was to make a strong case for its purposes.

"The People of"…Where?

The original Preamble proposed in August 1787 begins:

"We the People of the States of New Hampshire, Massachusetts, Rhode Island and Providence Plantations, Connecticut, New York, New Jersey, Pennsylvania, Delaware, Maryland, Virginia, North Carolina, South Carolina, and Georgia, do ordain, declare and establish the following Constitution for the Government of Ourselves and our Posterity."

Morris kept "We the People." Beyond that, the statements in the two versions are completely different.

When the delegates convened in Philadelphia in May, they came as representatives of their home states. By mid-September, the landscape inside the State House had changed. The Framers had formulated an overarching government. Morris recognized this development, deleted the names of the individual states from the first Preamble, and inserted the title of the country, capitalizing not only "States" but also "United."

When the Constitution was distributed for public scrutiny at state ratifying conventions, this last-minute switch caused a furor. Many people were not ready to transfer or even expand their allegiance from their beloved state to some large, hazy entity that didn't even exist yet.

❧ ❧

"I wish to know where they found the power…of consolidating the states."

—Joseph Taylor,

North Carolina Ratifying Convention

❧ ❧

Why were they so distressed?

The reason gets to a basic issue the Framers had wrestled with while writing the Constitution. Would the people who had won their independence from Great Britain four years earlier remain loyal to separate states, agreeing merely to join forces to resolve some gnarly problems? Or could they think of themselves as Americans?

Most importantly, would individual state governments or the federal government have more power? This debate echoes through the Constitution and the government the Framers created, and it still affects us today.

"We the People...In Order to..."

Despite these bitter differences of opinion, no one took issue with the phrase "We the people." It was a given that the people would govern themselves. They would not be ruled by a monarch who refused to let them decide things on their own.

But the Constitution left unclear exactly who "we the people" were. The Framers never defined the term, possibly because they might have disagreed. In 1787, women could not attend the Convention or run for election to any of the new offices. Neither could Native Americans or enslaved persons.

Only people like the Framers themselves—free, adult, white men who owned property or paid taxes—could participate in the government.

Nevertheless, no other country at the time was based on self-government. This was the revolutionary idea the Framers did agree on. This wholly new and newly empowered government was intended to establish a new society. The rest of the Preamble describes what they hoped that society would look like—the aims the Constitution was written "in order to" accomplish.

Morris didn't explain why he highlighted the particular desires inscribed in the Preamble, the resounding statement of the Framers' goals. The other Framers must have concurred, though, for they signed on to them with no discussion.

By looking at the daunting ordeals the country faced at the time, we can get an understanding of their meaning. At the same time, you might ponder whether they still mean the same to you.

15

SELLING THE CONSTITUTION

Once the Constitution was drafted, it was distributed to the states for discussion and approval. This process was called ratification. Hamilton, Madison, and John Jay (who called themselves Publius) wrote eighty-five essays, which they sent to newspapers. Arguing for the constitution, the essays became know as *The Federalist*.

The Framers decided that nine of the thirteen states would have to ratify the Constitution before it could go into effect. Voters in each state would choose delegates who would attend ratification conventions to determine the Constitution's fate.

Morris may have worried that the delegates might not agree to exchange the flawed but familiar Articles of Confederation for the unheard-of new arrangements. He probably penned the Preamble to make the Constitution more appealing. Who could turn down "the blessings of liberty"?

"Form a More Perfect Union"

To make sure "the people of the United States" understood the Framers' priorities, the Constitution notified them up front that they were merging into a single "union." This union would transform the separate states into one nation.

It would take effort to make the new system work. The people would have to agree to obey laws and pay taxes, imposed not only by their states but also by the new national government. They would have to accept an additional layer of leaders and decision makers above and distant from the ones they knew in their local capitals. They would have to stretch their loyalty from one state alone to the country as a whole.

If they did not, Thomas Jefferson wrote, "we may always be...an unimportant divided people." Actually, more like "peoples" than a single "we the people." But if everyone labored together for the good of all, the unification could succeed. They would accomplish the rest of the Preamble's goals.

"Establish Justice"

Surely a society should aim for justice. The Constitution tried to do this by creating a system of federal courts, which the Framers believed would protect citizens' rights better than the existing state courts.

Under the Articles of Confederation, the country's highest courts were at the state level. If someone in one state sued someone else in another, the judge might favor the person in his own state.

Federal judges, on the other hand, would be picked by the president, confirmed by the Senate, and paid by the national government, not the states. They would remain on the court for life, as long as they behaved themselves. As a result, they would be more likely to be impartial.

The Framers cared about a number of rights. Protecting property was an especially important one. But in most of the thirteen states, enslaved persons were considered property. Those who escaped from slave states to free states had to be returned to their owners. According to slave owners, that was the just thing to do. For abolitionists, that was the worst form of injustice.

The Framers disagreed fervently about slavery. Different—sometimes opposite—interpretations of "justice" led the delegates to make compromises and deals on this explosive issue. They hoped that courts would help enforce their compromises.

"Insure Domestic Tranquility"

America in the 1780s could be a tumultuous place to live. While Daniel Shays and his ragtag rebellious farmers caused mayhem in western Massachusetts, other states squabbled with each other.

• New York and New Hampshire tussled over their boundaries.

• Vermonters found both of these states so insufferable that they seceded from New York and New Hampshire, creating their own minuscule republic.

• Slave owners, especially in South Carolina where enslaved people were a majority of the population, feared that their chattel—human beings owned as property—would band together and revolt.

The Framers yearned for a national government that would ensure peace in the homeland.

"Provide for the Common Defense"

Internal strife wasn't the only source of hostilities during the late 1770s and 1780s. Along the vague outer boundaries of the thirteen states, enemies were often as close as the other side of a river or a disputed line scratched in the dirt.

Under the Articles of Confederation, Congress did not have the authority to raise an army to protect the inhabitants of any states. Far from being "common" (meaning "national"), defense against foreign intruders had to be conducted locally, militia by militia.

When forces from the Seneca Nation, defending their freedom, attacked families along New York's western borderline, that state's legislature rounded

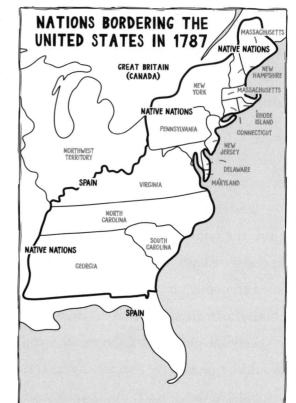

Great Britain—in the form of her province, Canada—lay just over the northern border.

Spain nudged both the southern side of Georgia and the western edge of Virginia from her vast holdings in what are now Florida, Louisiana, and beyond.

There was also the matter of the indigenous nations. As frontier families encroached on their lands after the Revolutionary War, both Great Britain and Spain supplied Native peoples with guns and gunpowder, which they used for raids on New York, Georgia, and the Carolinas.

up a thousand soldiers to guard it. All Congress could do was cheerlead from the sidelines by adopting a formal statement: "Resolved that Congress do approve of the spirited exertion of the said legislature…"

Even while the Constitutional Convention was meeting in June 1787, Virginia's Governor Beverley Randolph pleaded with the Confederation Congress to send either money or soldiers to defend his state's frontiers. Here is the response he received.

❧ ❧

"The misfortune is that there is no Congress at present to whom the application can be made; & if there was, I doubt much whether there would be a disposition in that body to incur any great expence for the security of an individual State. There are so many States…I doubt whether ever a shilling will be allowed."

—William Grayson, delegate to the Constitutional Congress, in a letter to Virginia Governor Beverley Randolph

❧ ❧

"Promote the General Welfare"

The Framers agreed that the new government should have the means to do what is necessary for the good of its citizens. They didn't specify what "the general welfare" meant beyond that, but they probably had several concerns in mind.

One was their desire to shift the mindset of the people from their state to the nation. When goods were sold across state lines, they were often advertised as being "imported," as if they had been brought in from another country. States charged tariffs on these "foreign" products. Eliminating these taxes would help the populace realize the states were part of a common country.

❧ ❧

"Just imported from Philadelphia… Dr. Martin's Celebrated Medicine for Cancers, Ulcers, Wens, Scurvies, Tatters, Ringworms, etc."

—advertisement in the *Columbian Herald*, Charleston, South Carolina, June 18, 1787

Another issue was the need to raise money to pay for roads and bridges, especially in the hinterlands to the west. About 80 percent of Americans lived in rural areas. Most roads consisted of dirt trails hacked through dense forests. The so-called Great Wagon Route meandered about four hundred miles between northern Virginia and Philadelphia. But it was often impassable because of deep mud, thick dust, herds of cattle, or broken-down wagons.

Farmers and merchants wanted their goods to reach markets reliably and quickly. The young country-on-the-move needed infrastructure and free passage of goods to promote its welfare.

"Secure the Blessings of Liberty to Ourselves and Our Posterity"

The Declaration of Independence states that liberty is one of mankind's "unalienable Rights," along with life and the pursuit of happiness. What liberties did the Framers want to secure—and how?

Liberty did not mean what we sometimes think of today: free rein to do whatever you want, with no limits. Just the opposite, in fact.

Liberty referred to freedom from rules imposed by a leader who wasn't chosen by the people, someone who could impose his will without consequence. There was one way to avoid a tyrant like that and to guarantee liberty: let the people rule themselves.

These new Americans, the Framers reasoned, wouldn't be free of rules; that would be uncivilized and chaotic. Instead, they would make and enforce the laws themselves. Or, at least, their chosen representatives would do so with the consent of the governed. In other words, self-government. That's the system the Framers intended their Constitution to establish—one that would ensure liberty forevermore.

TESTING THE CONSTITUTION

Just as the Preamble conveys the goals of the Constitution, this chapter provides the goal of the book—to judge how well the government established by the Constitution provides these benefits to Americans in the twenty-first century.

Through the amendment process, the Constitution has changed over time. So has our perception of the terms and concepts in the Preamble. Near the end we evaluate how well the Constitution has succeeded, using our understanding of the Framers' terms, in our times. We invite you to do the same, based on the meanings you assign to them.

PART I

How Bills Become
(Or, More Likely, Don't Become) Law

The Framers' Constitution set up a three-part government:

- a lawmaking legislature: Congress, which is divided into the Senate and the House of Representatives
- an executive branch: headed by the president
- a judicial branch: headed by the Supreme Court

This arrangement, called separation of powers, makes some sense. The checks and balances among the branches is similar to the rock-paper-scissors game in which each player has some power over the others but none can necessarily dominate the others.

But the structure can also cause turmoil that can be traced back to the Constitution. In this section, we look at several factors that too often cause our basic system to grind to a stop and lead to widespread unhappiness with the federal government. They include the following:

- the requirement that both houses of Congress must agree on every aspect of any bill in order for it to become a law
- the inequality built into the Senate
- the president's power to veto laws
- Senate rules that require supermajority votes—more than one-half plus one—for bills to be considered

CHAPTER 1

It Takes Two to Tango
Bicameralism

"Accosting a White Woman"

On August 11, 1913, Richard Puckett, a young black man from the small town of Laurens, South Carolina, found himself accused of "accosting a white woman" as she drove a buggy down a country road. Puckett denied the charge, and the woman did not identify him as the culprit. Nevertheless, he was jailed.

At 12:30 the next morning, a mob of about two thousand white men hauled Puckett from his cell, knotted a rope around his neck, and hanged him from a nearby railroad trestle. He was one of fifty-one black Americans known to have been lynched that year.

In 1918, Representative Leonidas C. Dyer introduced antilynching legislation

FROM 1877—1950
**4,384
BLACK PEOPLE
WERE
MURDERED
BY HANGING
99%
OF THE PERPETRATORS WENT
FREE
BECAUSE STATE AND LOCAL COURTS
FAILED TO PROSECUTE THEM**

into Congress. Dyer, a white man and a Republican from St. Louis, Missouri, was outraged about violence by white gangs against his black constituents. His bill intended to have people who were accused of lynching tried in federal court. Southerners in the House defeated the bill several times but it finally passed in 1922. President Warren G. Harding, a Republican, expressed his support.

Dyer's legislation then moved to the Senate for consideration. Southern members of that chamber, all of them Democrats, denounced the bill as an attack on the rights of states to deal with their lynchers however they saw fit, including doing nothing. Some went so far as to defend lynching as a way to protect white women from black men and to keep the races separate. To prevent the bill from ever coming up for a vote, a group of senators filibustered—that is, they talked on and on until it was clear they'd never stop. Dyer's measure failed.

A 1937 OPINION POLL FOUND THAT **72%** OF AMERICANS INCLUDING 57% OF SOUTHERNERS SUPPORTED ANTILYNCHING LAWS

ৡ ৶

"Whenever a Negro...
lays his black hand on a white woman,
he deserves to die."
—Democratic Senator James Thomas Heflin,
Alabama

ৡ ৶

Other representatives introduced similar bills in the 1930s and 1940s, possibly because Mexican-Americans were lynched as well as black people. Although they faced opposition too, the House passed three of these bills and sent them to the Senate for approval. Two were filibustered; the other was "passed over" three times through legislators' trickery.

Over the years, seven US presidents urged Congress to pass an antilynching law. No such bill had ever come up for a vote in the Senate, however, because members either filibustered or threatened to do so.

Meanwhile, Back in 1787…

The Articles of Confederation had established one legislative house consisting of representatives from each state to the Confederation Congress. However, while drafting a new Constitution, the Framers established a bicameral legislature. This meant that there were two chambers—the Senate and the House of Representatives. Both chambers would have to pass a bill before it could go to the president for his approval and become law.

❧ ❧

"All legislative Powers herein granted shall be vested in a Congress of the United States, which shall consist of a Senate and House of Representatives."

—Article I, Section 1

"Every bill which shall have passed the House of Representatives and the Senate, shall, before it become a law, be presented to the President of the United States."

—Article I, Section 7

❧ ❧

Why bother to have two houses? Wouldn't one be enough? And should each house have the power to kill legislation passed by the other?

The delegates to the Constitutional Convention were familiar with Britain's bicameral Parliament, which consisted

UNICAMERALS

In 1787, two states, Pennsylvania and Georgia, were unicameral—they had only one house. (Vermont did too, though it considered itself an independent country.)

Benjamin Franklin, a delegate to the Constitutional Convention from Pennsylvania, argued for a one-house Congress, but he was unsuccessful.

of the House of Lords and the House of Commons. Moreover, most of the American colonies had adopted bicameral governments when they became states after winning the Revolutionary War.

There was a problem, however, in translating the British practice to America. Members of the House of Commons were elected, though admittedly only approximately 10 percent of British citizens were entitled to vote. But the House of Lords were all aristocrats; no one voted for them. Their membership depended entirely on bloodlines; lords simply inherited their seats, usually from their fathers.

The Framers didn't want to mimic British society. They had renounced both the monarchy and an aristocracy in creating their new country.

෨ ෧

"No Title of Nobility shall be granted by the United States."

—Article I, Section 9

෨ ෧

The Declaration of Independence had called for "the consent of the governed." The Framers believed it was important to involve people in the government, so one chamber, the House of Representatives, would be the popular branch made up of relatively ordinary people elected by the voting public. But how would the other house be defined?

Since the Framers intended to ban aristocracy, they had no use for a house

THE GREAT BINDING LAW

As early as 1500, the five-nation Iroquois Confederacy developed oral laws that set up three bodies similar to an executive, a legislature, and a court system. Decisions were made by consensus among the nations' leaders, and treaties began "we the people." One of the Framers, John Rutledge of South Carolina, was friendly with a member of the Confederacy, a Mohawk named William Warraghiyagey Johnson. It is likely that some Framers knew of their arrangement and these words.

NAME THAT JOB!

The Framers went round and round on what to call the head of the government they were creating. One of the earliest drafts of the Constitution referred to him as the "National Executive." That was soon replaced with "Governor of the united People & States of America." Another version proposed, "His style shall be 'The President of the United States of America,' and his title shall be, 'His Excellency.'" The style stuck; the title did not.

When the government got rolling two years later, some officials still wanted to give him a title. Proposals included not only "Excellency" but also "Elective Highness," and "His Highness the President of the United States of America and Protector of Their Liberties." Vice President John Adams rejected "President" as demeaning because "there were presidents of fire companies." When he proposed that the president be called "His High Mightiness," jokesters referred to the portly Adams as "His Rotundity."

of lords. Nevertheless, they believed a second, upper house was necessary to keep an eye on the first. The Senate would be made up of upstanding, wealthy, educated members of society elected by state legislatures. James Madison of Virginia described them as "a more capable sett of men," who could be depended on to act "with more coolness, with more system, & with more wisdom, than the popular branch."

Today, we think of democracy as a good thing. At the time of the Constitutional Convention, however, "democracy" was not a term of praise. The Framers were uncomfortable with the prospect of untutored common folks—or the representatives they elected to the House—running the country, because they might run it right into the ground.

જી જી

"The people are…dupes."

—Governor Elbridge Gerry, Massachusetts

જી જી

The Senate, they believed, would protect the country from what Madison called the reckless "passions" of the people and an "excess of law-making." The Framers, therefore, erected hurdles that would make it hard to pass legislation that might arise from the people's unrestrained zeal without oversight from the Senate.

So What's the Big Problem?

A majority of the members of both houses of Congress must approve the exact same version of a bill for it to become law. This means that either body can block bills passed by the other. They have multiple ways to do so. Each can

- vote against a bill that the other house has passed;
- adopt rules that delay or prevent passage of bills;
- fail to bring a bill up for a vote;
- pass a bill that is very similar but not identical to a bill adopted in the first house. The two houses must come to precise agreement in order for a bill to move forward.

EXCEPTIONS TO BICAMERALISM

There are two exceptions to the general rule that both houses must agree before an action can be taken.

1. Only the Senate is involved in confirming presidential appointments, such as Supreme Court justices or heads of government agencies, called the cabinet; a majority vote is necessary.

2. Only the Senate ratifies treaties with other countries; two-thirds of the members must agree.

The versions can't differ by even a single word or comma!

Even if a hefty majority of the members of one house supports a piece of legislation, the bill might not get past the other house.

In 2010, for example, the public clamored for an overhaul of US immigration policies. With the support of both Republicans and Democrats, the Senate passed a bill that would have provided ways for almost all of the more than eleven million undocumented immigrants in the country to eventually become citizens. Some bipartisan support would have helped it get through the House of Representatives, too. But the Republican leader in the House opposed the bill and refused to bring it up for a vote.

Americans disagreed on whether it was a good or bad bill, but their representatives never had the chance to debate or vote on it. Gridlock over immigration continued to block action in Congress like a traffic jam, and almost everyone remained frustrated.

Political parties can make gridlock especially likely in a bicameral system. The Framers had hoped to stave off the formation of parties or factions. Most Framers believed that members of factions care only about what's good for their party or themselves—not what's good for the country. Nevertheless, parties triumphed. By 1796, there were two.

When one party controls one house of Congress and another party

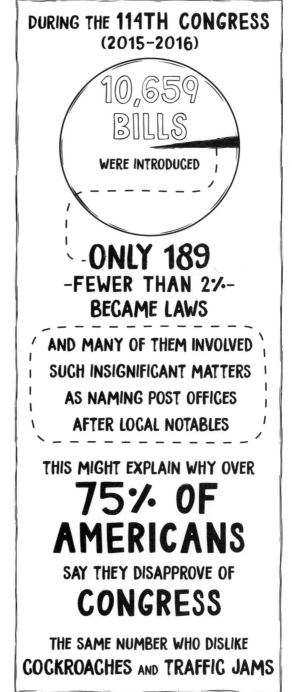

DURING THE **114TH CONGRESS**
(2015–2016)

10,659 BILLS

WERE INTRODUCED

ONLY 189
—FEWER THAN 2%—
BECAME LAWS

AND MANY OF THEM INVOLVED SUCH INSIGNIFICANT MATTERS AS NAMING POST OFFICES AFTER LOCAL NOTABLES

THIS MIGHT EXPLAIN WHY OVER
75% OF AMERICANS
SAY THEY DISAPPROVE OF
CONGRESS
THE SAME NUMBER WHO DISLIKE
COCKROACHES AND **TRAFFIC JAMS**

dominates the other house, business can grind to a halt if the members refuse to compromise on legislation. This can also happen even when the same party holds the majority of seats in both houses and sits in the Oval Office, if members can't come to agreement. In 2017, Republicans dominated the legislative and executive branches yet passed the fourth fewest bills in thirty years.

Judges sometimes say that it is better if juries allow ten guilty people to go free rather than send one innocent person to jail. Similarly, the Framers thought it would benefit the country as a whole if their new system let ten good—even necessary—laws fail rather than allow one terrible one to pass. The price we pay for checks and balances is logjam.

"...this complicated check on legislation may, in some instances, be injurious as well as beneficial."

—James Madison

There Are Other Ways
States

Nebraska has been the country's only unicameral state legislature since 1937. The state's legislators, called senators, are elected from districts of approximately equal population. But Nebraska is a relatively small state, with a population in 2018 of fewer than two million people. States of that size could probably operate just as well with one as with two separate houses.

"...there is no sense or reason in having the same thing done twice..."

—George Norris, Nebraska politician and advocate for a unicameral legislature

Other Countries

Many other countries have two legislative houses, but few allow one chamber to block a bill passed by the other chamber.

The power of the British House of

Lords over the House of Commons has been significantly limited since 1911. That year Parliament passed a law taking away the Lords' absolute veto over legislation. For instance, while the House of Lords can delay legislation passed by the House of Commons, it cannot squash it permanently.

France and Germany both allow their lower houses to enact legislation, under some circumstances, without the approval of the upper house.

In Norway, when the two houses disagree, they must meet together. If two-thirds of the combined members vote in favor of a law, then they can pass it.

These countries give greater authority to the "lower house" because it is thought to be closer to the people and, therefore, a better indicator of popular views.

The United States

Because the House of Representatives is supposed to more accurately reflect the will of the people than the Senate does,

perhaps the lower house should be able to pass legislation over the objection of the upper in some circumstances, just as in Britain, Germany, and France.

Or maybe we could try to adopt Norway's system. Then, if our two houses disagreed, the 435 members of the House would join with the 100 members of the Senate to create a temporary new body of 535 people. If two-thirds (358) of them agreed, they could pass a law.

The Story Continues

There is still no federal law against lynching. Nevertheless, one of the most remarkable events in the history of the United States Senate occurred on June 13, 2005, with the passage of Resolution 39.

Sponsored by eighty of the Senate's one hundred members, the Resolution "apologizes to the victims of lynching and the descendants of those victims for the failure of the Senate to enact anti-lynching legislation." The document noted that lynching was a "widely acknowledged practice in the United States until the middle of the 20th century," occurring in forty-six of the fifty states. Among the guests in the chamber that evening was Winona Puckett, Richard Puckett's niece.

In 2018, the Senate unanimously passed antilynching legislation introduced by three senators—two Democrats and a Republican. The House failed to take action before the end of the congressional session. The Senate passed the same legislation in 2019 and sent it to the House again.

❧ ❧

"There may be no other injustice in American history for which the Senate so uniquely bears responsibility."

—Senator Mary Landrieu, Louisiana

❧ ❧

CHAPTER 2

Big States, Little Say
The Senate

"Upside-Down Math"

Following the attacks of September 11, 2001, President George W. Bush asked Congress for laws and funds to track down terrorists and protect the American homeland.

Vermont's Democratic Senator Patrick J. Leahy, who was chairman of the Senate Judiciary Committee, called together House and Senate leaders and members of the president's staff to work on the legislation. He focused especially on how funding would be distributed to the states. As a representative from a small state, he wanted to be sure that his particular homeland would not be shortchanged.

On October 26, 2001, Congress passed the Uniting and Strengthening America by Providing Appropriate Tools Required to Intercept and Obstruct Terrorism (USA PATRIOT) Act. The legislation allocated $13.1 billion for states to detect and prevent local acts of terror. Leahy saw to it that the law mandated that every state, regardless of its size or need, would receive a minimum of 0.75 percent of the funds.

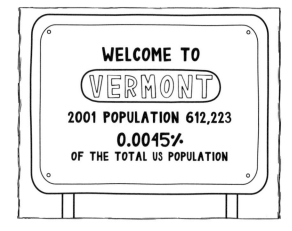

❧ ❧

"Whether it's a state of half a million or 4 million [people], you've got to do certain basic things."

—Senator Patrick Leahy, Vermont

❧ ❧

States used much of the money to hire more police, firefighters, and emergency workers as well as to buy equipment and pay for training to prevent and respond to potential terrorist attacks. States also sent the Department of Homeland Security (DHS) lists of sites they considered potentially appealing targets for terrorists. These lists helped DHS determine additional funding to protect those sites.

Places like the Hoover Dam and the Port of Los Angeles, for instance, were deemed high priorities for protection. Some of the smallest states, however, supplied the longest lists of possible targets, which upped their federal funding. Many of these, such as a petting zoo in Woodville, Alabama, and Amish

Country Popcorn in Berne, Indiana, seemed especially questionable. Even the shop's owner was perplexed as to why the state would cite his business "in the middle of nowhere" as a magnet for terrorists. "Maybe because popcorn explodes?" he suggested.

But the funding formula meant that the least money per resident went to the ten large states the Department considered the most likely targets of another terrorist attack. And the ten states at the bottom of the risk list—all of them small—received the highest amounts per resident. One report called this "the upside-down math of the new homeland-security funding."

❧ ❧

"We have big buildings you can put a lot of people in."

—Doug Friez, chief homeland security official, North Dakota
(ND received $52 per person, the fourth-highest allotment in the country)

❧ ❧

THE USA PATRIOT ACT FORMULA GAVE

WYOMING

$61 PER PERSON

BUT

CALIFORNIA

ONLY $14 PER PERSON

THE LOWEST AMOUNT OF ANY STATE

With the lopsided formula, small states had enough money left over, after meeting their security needs, to buy some dubious items:

- Colorado: fitness programs

- New Jersey: air-conditioned garbage trucks
- Washington, DC: a homeland security rap song

Bush encouraged Congress to revise the formula in order to send more money to states with high-risk large cities. But Leahy and his colleagues from rural states had a lot of leverage in the Senate. Because of the number of votes they could muster, they could hold hostage a bill they didn't like. A staffer said "World War III has broken out at meetings if we even talk about changing the formula."

How did small states start out with so much money compared to larger ones?

Meanwhile, Back in 1787...

On Wednesday, May 30, 1787, just three days after the delegates gathered in Philadelphia, they already faced a dilemma. How should the number of representatives to the upper house of the new national government be determined?

James Madison, representing the large state of Virginia, favored proportional representation: the bigger the population, the more votes it should have in both houses of Congress.

But when a resolution was introduced to establish that system, George Read, a delegate from tiny Delaware, declared that "it might become [our] duty to retire from the Convention." That is, Delaware threatened to walk out, a step that would torpedo a new constitution to replace the Articles of Confederation. This act would transform a dilemma into a full-scale crisis.

ೞ ☙

"Will not these large States crush the small ones… It seems as if Pa. & Va. by the conduct of their deputies wished to provide a system in which they would have an enormous & monstrous influence."

—Gunning Bedford, Delaware

Equal representation will "injure the majority of the people."

—James Madison, Virginia

ೞ ☙

In 1790, about 59,100 people lived in Delaware; of these, approximately 8,900 were enslaved. (No one at the Convention knew if or how enslaved people would be counted.) By comparison, about 434,300 people lived in Pennsylvania (3,700 or so enslaved). That's seven times the size of Delaware. And about 747,600 people, including about 292,000 enslaved people, lived in Virginia—twelve times the size of Delaware. Should small states have the same number of senators as big ones?

After cantankerous debate, everyone agreed to take a deep breath and adjourn to their rooming houses for the rest of the day.

On June 11, two delegates from Connecticut, Roger Sherman and Oliver Ellsworth, proposed a compromise—proportional representation in the lower house and equal representation in the

IN 1787
UNDER PROPORTIONAL REPRESENTATION

1/3 OF CONGRESS

WOULD COME FROM JUST

VIRGINIA AND PENNSYLVANIA

ONCE ANOTHER ONE OR TWO BIG STATES SENT THEIR REPRESENTATIVES TO THE CAPITOL,

THE SMALL ONES WOULD OFTEN HAVE NO INFLUENCE AT ALL

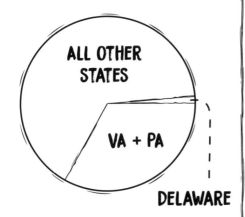

ALL OTHER STATES

VA + PA

DELAWARE

DELAWARE WOULD MAKE UP ONLY 1/90 OF THE GOVERNMENT

upper. Nasty arguments on both sides persisted.

James Wilson of Pennsylvania suggested that it would be fine with him if the small states pulled out of the union.

Gunning Bedford of Delaware retorted that, in that case, the small states would find another country to join. "I do not, gentlemen, trust you," he bellowed.

Distressed by "the small progress" they had made, Benjamin Franklin of Pennsylvania called for "prayers imploring the assistance of heaven." Alexander Hamilton was so discouraged that he went home to New York and wrote to George Washington that America might dissolve into "disunion, anarchy and misery." In response, Washington confessed he regretted going to Philadelphia because of the "deplorable state of things at the Convention." With other delegates threatening to stomp home, Gouverneur Morris of Pennsylvania said he fully expected the Convention to dissolve.

On July 2, Hugh Williamson of North Carolina pointed out, "If we do not concede on both sides, our business will soon be at an end."

Recognizing that Williamson was right, the group decided to let an eleven-person subcommittee come up with a compromise on representation. Then, despite the bitter feelings, they adjourned to celebrate July 4 together with gun salutes, displays of artillery and horse brigades, and fireworks. Still, the survival of the union was not a sure thing.

Two weeks later, on July 16, the subcommittee submitted its recommendation:

• The lower branch of the legislature, the House of Representatives, should be selected proportionally, according to the size of the state populations.

• The upper branch, the Senate, should contain the same number of representatives from each state.

With a margin of merely one vote, the Convention approved this so-called Great Compromise.

❧ ❧

"The House of Representatives shall be composed of Members chosen every second Year by the People of the several States."

—Article I, Section 2

❧ ❧

They still needed to determine how many senators each state would send to the Capitol. One seemed risky; if he got sick, the state wouldn't be represented at all. Three was too expensive. On July 23, the Constitutional Convention finally agreed on two.

❧ ❧

"The Senate of the United States shall be composed of two Senators from each State, chosen by the Legislature thereof, for six Years; and each Senator shall have one Vote."

—Article I, Section 3

❧ ❧

Still committed to a proportional system, Madison called the decision "a defeat, not [a] compromise." Nevertheless, he considered equal representation in the Senate a "lesser evil" than America's splintering into separate countries or remaining thirteen semi-independent states.

We live today with the result of this Great Compromise (also called the Connecticut Compromise) made at the Constitutional Convention. Though possibly "great," because it saved the union, it has also caused considerable injustice.

So What's the Big Problem?

Every congressional district contains roughly the same number of people—about 750,000 today. Larger states contain more districts and, therefore, send more members to the House of Representatives.

The Senate, on the other hand, is based on equal representation of the states, not the number of people. Each state, regardless of its size, elects two senators.

In 2018, less than half the people in

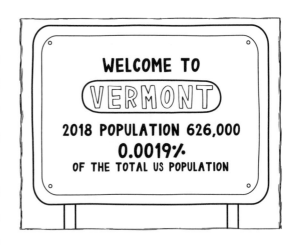

the country were spread across forty-one small states. With eighty-two senators, they had more than four times the pull in the Senate as all the others, who converged in just nine big states with larger cities and more diverse populations but only eighteen senators. This situation is likely to worsen. Forecasts indicate that in 2040, 70 percent of Americans will congregate in fifteen states, represented by only thirty senators. Unless another state joins the Union, the remaining 30 percent of the people will get the other seventy senators. That's topsy-turvy.

Senators from small states can secure more money per constituent from the federal government than can

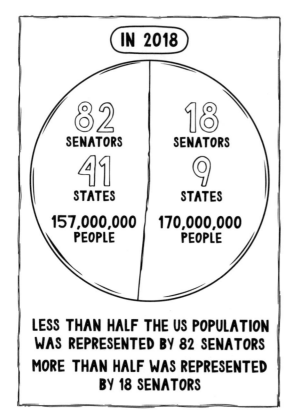

IN 2018

82
SENATORS
41
STATES
157,000,000
PEOPLE

18
SENATORS
9
STATES
170,000,000
PEOPLE

LESS THAN HALF THE US POPULATION
WAS REPRESENTED BY 82 SENATORS
MORE THAN HALF WAS REPRESENTED
BY 18 SENATORS

those from larger ones. Leahy had the power to get extra money for Vermont because he, along with his small-state colleagues, controlled enough votes to demand it.

Researchers point out that this arrangement of equal representation in the Senate has even affected snacks and school lunches—as well as the rising number of obese Americans. The five farm-based states of the upper Midwest (Iowa, Kansas, Minnesota, and the two Dakotas) hold 10 percent of the Senate, though only 4 percent of the US population. Since the 1930s, rural senators have persuaded Congress to pass farm bills that encourage farmers to grow certain crops by giving them subsidies—money to buy seeds, for instance. This helps their constituents.

Funding formulas change but the crop for which farmers have received the most subsidies over the years is corn. So, corn appears in feed for cattle and hogs (making meat more caloric) and high-fructose corn syrup (a high-calorie ingredient in soft drinks and many processed foods).

Even worse, farmers who accept subsidies are urged to use only 15 percent of their acreage to plant fruits and other vegetables, making these healthier crops more expensive. As a result, calorie for calorie, corn chips cost less than carrots.

"Taxpayers are paying for the privilege of making our country sick," one study concluded.

The problem with having a Senate that doesn't represent the population

IN 2014, TOTAL FEDERAL AID TO STATE BUDGETS MEANT THAT

RECEIVED
$1,549 PER RESIDENT
BUT

VERMONT

RECEIVED
$3,091 PER RESIDENT
THAT'S
TWICE
AS MUCH!

THAT MUCH MONEY CAN TRANSLATE TO BETTER ROADS, NEWER BRIDGES, AND MORE HOMELAND SECURITY IN RURAL AREAS THAN IN URBAN CENTERS

racially diverse and more politically conservative than states with big cities. Here are two examples.

• About 90 percent of all Americans—including almost 75 percent of the members of the National Rifle Association—favor background checks of people who want to buy guns. Nevertheless, there are enough senators from states with low populations, who prefer unchecked gun ownership, to prevent such legislation from passing.

• A majority of the Senate, representing a minority of Americans, can confirm or reject federal judges, including those on the Supreme Court. Judges serve for life but might not have the support of most voters.

Madison was right: equal representation does injure the majority of the people.

There Are Other Ways
States

as a whole isn't limited to money. It also skews policies. Senators from large states have to pay attention to more issues back home than do those from small states. In addition, rural states that have few people but, when combined, a lot of senators tend to be less

Many American states initially modeled themselves after the national government

AMERICAN (CHILDREN)

CONSUME AN AVERAGE OF AN EXTRA

130 CALORIES A DAY OF CORN-BASED DRINKS

THAT COULD AMOUNT TO OVER

13 POUNDS OF WEIGHT GAINED EVERY YEAR, ON TOP OF NORMAL GROWTH

(ADULTS)

WHO CONSUME THE MOST

SUBSIDIZED FOODS

HAVE A FAR HIGHER RISK OF BECOMING

OBESE

and established bicameral legislatures in which the upper house was like the Senate. In these states, each county or district had equal representation, regardless of population. Some people referred to this system at the state level as "little federalism," with "big federalism" being the national government.

This practice came to an end in 1964, when the Supreme Court said that "little federalism" was unconstitutional because it violated "equal protection of the laws." This phrase means that all people should be treated fairly. It became part of the Constitution when the Fourteenth Amendment was ratified in 1868.

The Supreme Court used this principle in a case called *Reynolds v. Sims*, in which M. O. Sims sued the state of Alabama. He claimed that he was not fairly represented in the state senate because the district where he lived had fourteen times as many people as another one.

The court agreed with Sims, declaring that he was not receiving equal protection of the laws. The decision applied to all fifty states.

Even more dramatic was Vermont's General Assembly, where the smallest district contained only thirty-six people and the largest thirty-five thousand!

Both houses of every state legislature, the court ruled, had to be elected on the basis of what the court called "one-person/one-vote"; every district has to have roughly equal population. This formula makes as much sense for the US government as it does for states. There are only two reasons the court didn't apply this view to the US Senate:

• The Great Compromise, which embedded equal representation in the Constitution, wouldn't allow it.

• The Equal Protection Clause refers only to states, not the national government.

Other Countries

Many countries have bicameral legislatures. Some, such as Switzerland and Australia, also have uneven representation in one of their chambers, just like the United States. What makes the United States exceptional is the extent of the variation in population between the smallest and the largest states.

On top of that, in many other countries, the chamber that is more representative of the people has more power than the one that is not. For instance, in at least five countries—Austria, the Czech Republic, France, Poland, and Spain—the upper house generally cannot kill laws passed by the lower house. This is different from the United States, where the House and Senate have equal influence on legislation.

The ways that members of the upper house are selected in other countries also differ from ours. In Australia, each of the six states is represented by twelve senators, who are elected by proportional representation. In addition, the Australian National Territory, where the capital, Canberra, is located, and the Northwest Territory each get two senators. This system makes it easy for small parties to win a seat. As a result, there is a greater variety of viewpoints in the upper house than the lower one.

The United States

Even if equal rather than proportional voting power by the states were a good idea, a question remains. Were the Framers wise to specify two senators per state in the Constitution? Instead, they might have declared that each state have an equal number of senators, to be determined by Congress.

Since 1959, when Hawaii became the last state to join the union, we have had a total of one hundred members of the Senate. But the national population has almost doubled since then.

Moreover, today Congress confronts many more issues than was the case even in 1960, let alone earlier in our history. Maybe it would have been a good idea to increase the number of senators to three or four as both the country's population and the issues facing Congress grew. That way, they could share the duties of attending committee hearings, learning about complicated new issues, keeping in touch with constituents, and participating in debates on the Senate floor.

But why elect senators only from states? Additional senators could be elected from broader geographical regions of the country. Or perhaps former presidents, vice presidents, or retired members of the Supreme Court could serve in the Senate. The Senate would be bigger and so would the scope of what they pay attention to—not just what their constituents want but what's best for the whole country.

The Story Continues

In 2007, then-Senator Barack Obama supported a bill that decreased the minimum grant to every state from 0.75 percent of PATRIOT Act funds to 0.25 percent. This bill died. To steer more money to the areas most at risk of terrorism and violence when he became president, Obama directed the Department of Homeland Security to award funds from various programs to states along America's vulnerable borders and to urban areas. Using a calculation based on the likelihood of threats, the Department did so. Nevertheless, Wyoming still gets more money per person from the PATRIOT Act than California does.

CHAPTER 3

Delete!
Presidential Veto

"The Morally Right Thing to Do"

In January 2004, Paula and Jeff Novak of Lebanon, Ohio, welcomed their third son into the family. Seth was born with Down syndrome, and, like many infants with this condition, he needed open-heart surgery, genetic and hormone testing, eye and ear exams, special footwear, and speech therapy.

For several years the Novaks could afford these essential but costly services because of a federal insurance program called Medicaid, which uses state and federal funds to help low-income families with medical expenses. But when Jeff got a raise, they lost their Medicaid coverage. Every other insurance program they looked into labeled Seth uninsurable because of his condition.

Fortunately, less than a year later, Ohio Governor Ted Strickland approved a budget that allowed families like the Novaks to receive Medicaid, even if their incomes rose slightly. Paula said they felt privileged that Seth could once again see the doctors and therapists he needed.

Then the president stepped in. On August 17, 2007, President George W. Bush directed the states to limit who could be covered by Medicaid. He believed that the program should support only very poor people and that the federal government should not cover those who were merely low income.

Congress disagreed. To overcome the president's order, both the House and the Senate introduced bills to expand funding for a joint federal-state program called the State Children's Health Insurance Program (SCHIP). SCHIP would cover another estimated four million uninsured children—including Seth. With support from both Republicans and Democrats, the legislation passed overwhelmingly and was sent to the president for his signature.

Bush vetoed the bill. Congress was outraged. Republican Senator Orrin Hatch of Utah stated that supporting a health bill for children was "the morally right thing to do."

MEDICAID AND CHIP

Medicaid provides basic medical coverage for poor and nearly poor children and, in some states, their parents as well as other low-income adults needing services.

SCHIP, now called CHIP, covers children whose parents earn too much to qualify for Medicaid but do not have private health insurance.

Bush has made "an irresponsible use of the veto pen."

—Republican Senator Gordon Smith, Oregon

"One of the things the president can do is say, 'I'm not going to sign a bill that...has policies in it that should not be a part of the United States policy.'"

—Dana Perino, White House spokeswoman

The president would not necessarily have the last word. Senators and representatives committed to SCHIP could override Bush's veto if at least two-thirds of the members of each house voted to do so. The bill had already passed the Senate by that margin, but getting it through the House, where opinions were more evenly split, was more problematic.

When the bill came up for vote again, it passed with 273 members in favor and 156 opposed. This result showed overwhelming support—but not by the necessary two-thirds majority. Congress sent a revised bill to Bush but he vetoed it as well. After that, Congress gave up.

Seth and approximately four million other low-income kids remained uninsured.

Meanwhile, Back in 1787...

As Americans designed a government for themselves, they had to decide how powerful they wanted their new president to be in comparison to the legislature and the courts. The Framers quarreled for three months, longer than for any other issue, over the powers the president should—and should not—have.

Some of the Framers pointed out that the colonists' very first complaint against King George III in their Declaration of Independence was that he overruled laws passed by the colonial legislature.

❧ ❧

"He has refused his Assent to Laws, [which are] the most wholesome and necessary for the public good."

—Declaration of Independence

❧ ❧

Yet as supporters of the Revolution, the Framers had also been critical of King George when he did not veto laws passed by the British Parliament that colonists considered unconstitutional.

Even those who believed that the president should stay out of Congress's way thought he should be allowed to veto bills he considered unconstitutional. He would take an oath, after all, to "preserve, protect and defend the Constitution." Wouldn't this require the president to refuse to sign legislation he thought contradicted the Constitution?

Some delegates believed this presidential veto power should extend also to unwise legislation, even if it was perfectly constitutional. Alexander Hamilton of New York would have happily given the president an absolute veto, which Congress could not override. This view was remarkable since only two states allowed their governors to veto laws passed by the legislature.

༖ ༅

"The most virtuous Citizens will often as members of a legislative body concur in measures which afterwards in their private capacity they will be ashamed of."

—Gouverneur Morris, Pennsylvania

༖ ༅

Pierce Butler of South Carolina, on the other hand, argued that such a veto might turn the president into a dictator. The Framers wanted to prevent that from happening, but clashed on whether overturning a presidential veto should require agreement from two-thirds or three-quarters of the members of each house. Fearing that, if they couldn't make up their minds, they'd be stuck in Philadelphia until the end of the year, they narrowly opted for three-quarters.

Two weeks later and just days before adjourning, they changed their minds and switched to two-thirds. We continue to operate under the terms of their last-minute flip-flop.

༖ ༅

"Every Bill which shall have passed the House of Representatives and the Senate, shall, before it become a Law, be presented to the President of the United States: If he approve he shall sign it, but if not he shall return it, with his Objections to that House in which it shall have originated, who shall enter the Objections at large on their Journal, and proceed to reconsider it. If after such Reconsideration two thirds of that House shall agree to pass the Bill, it shall be sent, together with the Objections, to the other House, by which it shall likewise be reconsidered, and if approved by two thirds of that House, it shall become a Law..."

—Article I, Section 7

༖ ༅

So What's the Big Problem?

The executive branch, which is supposed to be a separate power from the legislative branch, often inserts itself into the lawmaking process, which many people believe is Congress's responsibility. The mere threat of a presidential veto can force Congress to change a bill before sending it to the White House. This is especially likely to happen when the government is divided—that is, when one political party has the majority in Congress but the president belongs to the other party.

For a bill to become a law, it must receive support from a majority of the members of each house of Congress who are present and voting before it goes to the president for signature. But that doesn't necessarily mean it will become a law. The president can still veto it, even if most of the elected representatives of the people voted for it. There are two ways this can occur:

• The president can refuse to sign a bill that reaches the Oval Office within ten days before the end of the legislative session. This is called a pocket veto. These days, Congress is in session practically year-round, so pocket vetoes are unlikely.

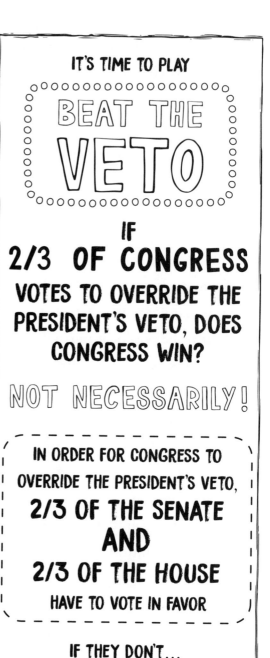

IT'S TIME TO PLAY

BEAT THE VETO

IF 2/3 OF CONGRESS VOTES TO OVERRIDE THE PRESIDENT'S VETO, DOES CONGRESS WIN?

NOT NECESSARILY!

IN ORDER FOR CONGRESS TO OVERRIDE THE PRESIDENT'S VETO, 2/3 OF THE SENATE AND 2/3 OF THE HOUSE HAVE TO VOTE IN FAVOR

IF THEY DON'T...

PRESIDENT WINS!

• Far more commonly, the president returns a bill to the house that first proposed it, unsigned but with an explanation of why he refused to sign it. In this case, Congress must vote on it again. But this time around, its supporters have to round up a two-thirds majority in each house to overcome the president's veto.

Because of the president's power to overturn popular bills, we have, in effect, what John Adams called a tricameral—three-part—legislature.

In 1971, Congress, which was held by Democrats, passed a program to establish childcare centers for working parents. This could have meant day care, meals, and medical checkups for children of needy families, with fees based on the parents' incomes. President Richard M. Nixon, who was Republican, vetoed the idea, saying that families, not government, should raise children. Congress couldn't muster the required votes to beat back his veto.

In 1990, President George H. W. Bush vetoed a civil rights bill that would have banned racial discrimination in hiring and promoting workers. Supporters of the bill in the Senate tried to round up the necessary votes again. But, they could count on only sixty-six votes, not the sixty-seven needed to override the president's veto. The bill failed by one vote.

Of course, Democrats veto highly popular bills, too. In 1997, President Bill Clinton vetoed legislation regarding late-term abortions. The House handily overrode his veto with the necessary supermajority of 296 to 132. The Senate fell three votes short of doing so with a tally of 64 to override to 36. The president won.

The year before, Congress had voted to give Clinton (and all succeeding presidents) authority for "line-item" vetoes under certain circumstances. This would allow him to delete bits and pieces of a bill and approve the rest. But in 1998, the Supreme Court ruled that line-item vetoes were unconstitutional. The justices interpreted the Constitution as requiring an all-or-

FROM 1789 TO 2017

44 PRESIDENTS VETOED

2,574 BILLS

ONLY 111 - -

OVERCAME THE SUPERMAJORITY BARRIER AND BECAME LAW

THAT'S JUST 4%!

nothing decision by the president, with no picking and choosing allowed.

Voters who are generally satisfied with the country the way it is might approve of our system because it makes it difficult to pass laws. On the other hand, those who would like the government to be more active might prefer fewer roadblocks to passing new laws.

Almost everyone agrees that some

laws should be vetoed. But since George Washington's day, presidents have vetoed more than 2,500 bills that Congress passed. Should there be so many hurdles in the way of congressional majorities?

There Are Other Ways
States

The executives—that is, governors—of all fifty states can veto laws their legislature sends them, but the process varies.

Most states follow the federal practice of requiring a supermajority—two-thirds of their state legislators—to override the governor's veto. Alabama, Arkansas, Indiana, Kentucky, Tennessee and West Virginia, on the other hand, allow a majority of the legislature's members to override a veto.

In North Carolina, the governor had no veto power at all until 1996. Now, three-fifths of the members of the North Carolina House and Senate must vote to override the governor's veto.

All but six governors can veto specific sections of a bill without vetoing all of it. The president does not have this right to a line-item veto.

Other Countries

Many different versions of executive veto systems are practiced around the world.

The president of Switzerland cannot veto any laws passed by the Federal Assembly, the country's legislature.

The president of Cyprus can veto any piece of legislation relating to foreign affairs, defense, and security, and cannot be overruled.

The president of South Africa can send a bill back to the lower house, which is called the National Assembly but only if he believes it is unconstitutional and explains why. If the Assembly disagrees and readopts the bill unchanged, it goes to the South African Constitutional Court, a special court charged with assessing the constitutionality of legislation. If the court agrees with the Assembly that the legislation is constitutional, then the president must sign it.

The United States

There are two ways to make it easier to pass laws, if you think that's a good idea:

- Eliminate the president's right to veto bills passed by Congress.
- Or lower the percentage of votes necessary to overcome a veto to a simple majority.

Making either of these changes would mean amending the Constitution.

The Story Continues

In January 2009, just after the inauguration of President Barack Obama, Congress adopted a bill to expand medical care for kids, including CHIP. The president signed it, ensuring continued funding into 2017. After months of delay, Congress extended CHIP in early 2018 for six years. President Donald J. Trump then proposed a budget maneuver to cut $7 billion from the program; nevertheless, children will retain their health insurance.

CHAPTER 4

Majority Rules—Except When It Doesn't
Supermajority Rules

"You Don't Have Papers"

Leezia Dhalla, a journalism major at Northwestern University in Chicago, was ecstatic in the fall of 2010 when a major newspaper, the *Dallas Morning News*, awarded her a competitive internship—for pay!—after her graduation the following summer. A member of her high school's Model United Nations program, the debate team, the school paper, and the National Honor Society, Dhalla had prepared for this job practically her whole life—or at least since she and her parents had immigrated to the United States from Canada when she was six years old.

But a troublesome wrinkle arose. Dhalla, who is Muslim, was not an American citizen; she carried a Canadian passport. To receive a salary, she needed a work permit. She had applied for one but it had never arrived. The editor rescinded the job offer.

"I was crushed," Dhalla said. "I wanted that internship more than anyone I knew."

Losing the job, though, turned out to be the least of her problems. When she came home for vacation in mid-December her father handed her a letter. The Department of Homeland Security demanded that she appear in immigration court—the first step in a process that can result in deportation from the United States. But why, she wondered? She'd been in the country all these years on a visa with no problems.

At that point her father finally had to tell her, "You don't have papers." Dhalla was stunned. Unknown to her, the family had stayed longer than their visas allowed. She was in the country illegally.

Suddenly details of her childhood made sense. No wonder her parents hadn't allowed her to apply for a driver's license or study overseas. If she got into an accident, she could be expelled. If she traveled out of the country, she couldn't return. And that's why, the day before, her mother had mentioned a bill coming up for a vote in Congress.

The bill, called the Development, Relief and Education for Alien Minors (DREAM) Act, was first introduced in Congress in 2001, and Dhalla's parents fervently hoped it would pass. This bill offered young undocumented residents who had entered the United States before the age of sixteen a way to eventually become citizens, as long as they passed a background check, paid a fine, and remained in good standing for over

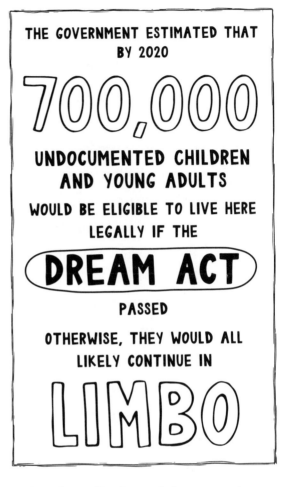

THE GOVERNMENT ESTIMATED THAT BY 2020 **700,000** UNDOCUMENTED CHILDREN AND YOUNG ADULTS WOULD BE ELIGIBLE TO LIVE HERE LEGALLY IF THE **DREAM ACT** PASSED OTHERWISE, THEY WOULD ALL LIKELY CONTINUE IN **LIMBO**

a decade. Polls showed that most Americans supported the legislation.

Opponents vowed to defeat the DREAM Act, charging that the bill would give amnesty to criminals. Nevertheless, with bipartisan support in both houses, there was a strong chance the legislation would succeed.

On December 9, 2010, the DREAM Act passed the House with 216 representatives voting in favor and 198 against. This was a narrow but clear majority.

Now the bill just needed to slide through the Senate. Following a week of debate, fifty-five senators—more than half—voted for the bill. A majority of Congress had supported the DREAM Act.

Yet on December 18, it failed to pass.

How could a bill that had the solid support of the majority of both houses of Congress die? The Senate's vote on the DREAM Act wasn't really on the bill itself. Under Senate rules, the group first had to vote on whether to end their debate and then vote on the bill. A majority wanted to—but not a supermajority, which Senate rules required. Debate was over. So were the DREAM Act and Dhalla's hopes of working in America without constant fear of deportation.

Meanwhile, Back in 1787...

If the Framers had dealt with every possible issue, the Constitution would have been unbearably long and, as one of them said, "clogged." The House and Senate would need to adopt rules so they could operate efficiently and fairly. Trusting that they would do so, the Framers let the House and the Senate figure out their own rules. There was no discussion about this either at the Convention or during the ratification debates afterward.

࿇ ࿇

"Each House may determine the Rules of its Proceedings…"

—Article I, Section 5

࿇ ࿇

The Framers probably presumed that Congress's rulebook would be based on majority decision-making. It's likely that's the reason the Constitution writers spelled out exceptions to majority rule.

❧ ❧

"...the American system of government
requires that the sense
of the majority should prevail."

—Alexander Hamilton, New York

❧ ❧

In 1917, the Senate adopted Rule XXII, which described the process of breaking a filibuster and allowing a bill to come up for a vote. This process, called "invoking cloture" (*clôture* is a French word meaning "closure"), initially required two-thirds of the members to agree to end debate. That percentage was immensely difficult to achieve. If every member of the Senate was present, sixty-four members out of a total of ninety-six at the time had to vote to invoke cloture. In 1975, they reduced the fraction to three-fifths (now sixty of one hundred members), which is still difficult to reach.

The Senate has other responsibilities besides passing—or blocking—bills. The Framers also gave this body the

LOTS OF RULES!

Currently the Senate has forty-four Standing Rules, covering subjects like

- the order in which to read memorials about deceased citizens,
- circumstances when the sergeant at arms can compel the attendance of absent senators, and
- ethical violations.

The House has twenty-nine Standing Rules, covering subjects like

- limiting each member's speech to five minutes at a time and therefore prohibiting filibusters,
- setting procedures for electing officers,
- establishing committees to study bills, and
- determining the days of the week certain issues will be considered.

job of approving the president's nominees for federal judges, including the Supreme Court.

෨ ෨

"[The President]…shall nominate, and by and with the Advice and Consent of the Senate, shall appoint…Judges of the supreme Court, and all other Officers of the United States…"

–Article II, Section 2

෨ ෨

Senators can filibuster just about anything they choose.

So What's the Big Problem?

Beginning in the twentieth century, filibusters often brought Senate business to a complete halt, particularly when legislation dealt with civil rights. Nothing else got done as senators droned on or harangued each other. Speeches lasted through the night; cots were brought to the floor.

Filibusters—often politely referred to as extended debate—were powerful tools because they took up so much time that they disrupted the Senate's ability to do its other work. Senate Rule

---

INFAMOUS FILIBUSTERERS

The record for the longest filibuster belongs to Senator Strom Thurmond of South Carolina, who protested the Civil Rights Act of 1957 for twenty-four hours and eighteen minutes.

A fictional filibuster of that length was portrayed in a 1939 movie, *Mr. Smith Goes to Washington*, about a naïve but honest newcomer to the Senate who speaks against a corrupt bill. Mr. Smith won. Mr. Thurmond lost.

Senator Ted Cruz of Texas came close to the record in 2013 when he took over the Senate floor for more than twenty-one hours to gripe about the Affordable Care Act, which was already a law. During the evening, he read a Dr. Seuss story in case his daughters were watching him on C-SPAN.

XXII attempted to resolve this obstacle but rarely succeeded.

As a result, the fate of a bill can boil down to whether to end debate, not on whether a majority agrees with the policy. That's what happened to the DREAM Act. Only fifty-five senators

WHAT HAPPENS TO A BILL WHEN **THE SENATE DISAGREES?**

IF

,60 OF 100, SENATORS,

(A SUPERMAJORITY)

AGREE TO END DISCUSSION

THE BILL COMES UP FOR A VOTE

IF

,41 OF 100, SENATORS,

(A FILIBUSTER)

REFUSE TO END DISCUSSION

THE BILL NEVER COMES UP FOR A VOTE

JUST THE **THREAT** OF A **FILIBUSTER** CAN PREVENT A BILL FROM COMING UP FOR A VOTE

—more than a majority but less than a supermajority—voted to close debate, dooming it to oblivion.

What used to be exceptional—the minority party filibustering a bill to stop it in its tracks—became ordinary. In the decade between 2007 and 2017, at least 788 bills were filibustered to death. And these are just the ones we know about. Others were certainly smothered by threats made behind closed doors. Rules now allow senators to call for a filibuster without having to be present.

This tactic can be very frustrating for senators and their constituents. With the two major political parties increasingly at odds with each other, it has become nearly impossible to persuade three-fifths of the Senate to agree on anything controversial. That includes not only legislation but also judges the president wants to appoint. After all, federal judges rule on what the Constitution means, and they can remain on the bench for life.

Democrats were especially vexed during President Barack Obama's administration when Republicans refused to take action on his nominees to the federal courts. In 2013, Democrats, who were in the majority, voted to change Senate rules, ending the filibuster for almost all presidential nominations. The only exception was for Supreme Court justices. That allowed them to approve many of the president's judicial appointments.

Four years later, Republicans were in charge. They refused to even hold hearings in 2016, when President Obama nominated Merrick Garland to the top court. Then, when Democrats attempted to filibuster President Donald J. Trump's nominee, Judge Neil Gorsuch, Republicans in the Senate wiped off the books the section of Rule XXII regarding that court. This action was so dramatic, it was called the nuclear option.

Defenders of the filibuster argue that it helps prevent tyranny of the majority, that is, the ability of those in charge to ignore the needs and opinions of minorities. Opponents counter that the majority should rule, no matter what. Trump tweeted as much in May 2017: "...change the rules now to 51%." The filibuster remains very controversial.

There Are Other Ways
States
Half the states require a supermajority vote in their legislatures to take action only on specific items, generally related to budget or taxes. Otherwise, in those and in the remaining states, majority vote is sufficient to carry out business.

Until 2015, the Texas Senate required that two-thirds of its members must agree to bring a bill up for a vote; otherwise, it would be shelved. This arrangement gave clout to the minority party but was eliminated when the dominant party, the Republicans, no longer wished to share power.

Filibusters at the state level are rare, though not unknown. House Democrats in Colorado filibustered a bill about charter schools proposed by a member of their own party in 2017. In most state legislatures, the party in power can end debate. Some of these states require an absolute majority—that is, a majority of the entire membership—to end debate, while others accept a majority of only those legislators who are present and voting.

Other Countries

Ordinary legislation generally requires only majority approval. A handful of countries require supermajority support for certain actions, such as proposals for constitutional amendments. For instance, legislators in India and Japan cannot amend their constitutions without agreement from at least two-thirds of their members.

As for filibusters, some countries allow members to delay votes, but not to block them as members are able to in the United States Senate.

In Japan, resisters can resort to *ushi aruki*, meaning "cow-walking." They can take hours to get from their seat to the ballot box twenty feet away but eventually they make it and have to vote.

The British Parliament allows members to speak for a maximum of four hours, and they must stay on topic.

The United States

Senators can still filibuster bills. But by a majority vote, they could delete this final bit of Rule XXII, the same way they eliminated the filibuster for judgeships. Ordinary legislation could then be passed by a majority of the Senate rather than needing a supermajority to get to a vote at all. For better or worse, the Senate might take this step at any time.

Alternatively, the Constitution could be amended. This strategy would allow the supermajority requirement to stand in regard to voting on treaties and other areas where the government might want more than half of the elected officials to agree before they take effect.

The Story Continues

In 2012, President Obama issued an executive order called Deferred Action for Childhood Arrivals (DACA). This policy allows certain undocumented immigrants who had entered the United States as minors to apply every two years to postpone deportation and to receive a work permit.

One of the requirements is that

applicants must have arrived in the country before the program was announced—June 15, 2012. Since that was the day Dhalla graduated from college, she provided graduation photos as proof. Thanks to DACA, she has been able to work legally—focusing on immigration reform—both in Texas and in Washington, DC.

In 2017, President Trump threatened to end DACA, though Congress did not take action. Lawsuits both supporting DACA and trying to kill it have been filed in various federal courts. In November 2018, a court ruled that Trump cannot stop DACA. This decision means that the Supreme Court will probably decide whether the program lives or dies.

If it goes down, Dhalla could be deported to Canada, even though she has not visited the country since she was six years old. In any case, her status expires in 2020. Meanwhile, she and hundreds of thousands of other young undocumented immigrants remain in limbo.

ॐ ॐ

"I consider myself American in every way except on paper. Every day it's in the back of your mind. Every day, you wonder if it will be the last time you see your parents."

—Leezia Dhalla

ॐ ॐ

PART II

Hello, Can You Hear Me?

There are many ways in which our Constitution makes it difficult—sometimes even impossible—for citizens to participate in the democratic process. Built-in requirements give states the power to decide who can vote and to restrict who can run for certain political offices. These limitations raise important questions and point to fault lines in our "representative government."

This section looks at

- how the size and shape of congressional districts are determined,
- why the District of Columbia is not represented in Congress, and
- who does—and who does not—get to participate in decision-making.

CHAPTER 5

How to Cherry-pick Voters
Gerrymandering

"Doggett Is Unacceptable"

Lloyd Doggett, an Anglo Democrat from Austin, Texas, just might be the most nimble member of Congress. First elected in 1994 from a safely Democratic district, he was easily reelected four times. But then the political landscape changed.

The Constitution lets every state decide on the process for determining the shape and location of its federal congressional districts. States generally draw these district maps once every ten years, following the most recent US census. This population survey determines which states have gained or lost residents and therefore the number of representatives each will send to Congress.

In Texas, as is the case in most states, the legislature draws the maps for congressional districts. These maps determine the geographical boundaries of each district. When legislators draft them, they can shift the boundary lines around to include—and exclude—certain populations. The Supreme Court requires that each district contain roughly the same number of individuals, but each district's shape and location are left up to elected state senators and representatives.

Politicians look closely at who lives within a district when they are considering possible boundary lines. They want to know whether the residents are generally

- well-off or poor;
- Anglo, Hispanic, African-American, or another minority group; and, most importantly,
- registered Democrats, Republicans, or Independents.

This information indicates how the residents are likely to vote in upcoming elections. State legislators can use such data to control the makeup of the districts.

From 1995, when he took office, through 2002, most of Doggett's constituents were Democrats who, like him, lived in Austin, the state capital. That's because the state legislators who drew the district maps were mostly Democrats who had configured the districts in their own favor. They made sure Doggett's district was largely composed of his supporters.

In 2000, though, there was a balance of power between Democrats and Republicans in the state. And the "lege," as Texans call their senators and representatives in Austin, couldn't agree on a plan. So a state court came up with one. Doggett was able to keep his familiar

seat. He hoped fervently that this would remain the case until at least 2011, following the 2010 census.

But public opinion and party membership in the state shifted dramatically during the early 2000s. After statewide elections in 2002, both the legislature and the governor's mansion were in the hands of Republicans. It was time for payback, and the Republicans wanted to replace Doggett—along with nine other Texas Democrats—with congresspeople from their own party. Doggett was a prominent, outspoken, liberal representing a city whose slogan read "Keep Austin Weird."

To make sure they would win seats in the House of Representatives in the very next election—and Doggett would lose his—in 2003, the Republicans rejiggered the court's plan. A staffer even wrote in a memo, "We must stress that a map that returns…Doggett [to office] is unacceptable." They almost succeeded in tossing him out.

Rather than retaining a district composed mostly of Democratic residents in Austin, Doggett was placed in a skinny new district that began with a sliver of Austin in the north and zig-zagged 225 miles south to the Mexico border. Because of its shape, locals called this region the Fajita Strip. Doggett's enemies assumed that voters in this new district, many of whom were Hispanic, would choose a Hispanic candidate in the Democratic primary instead of Doggett. They figured that enough Republicans lived in the district to defeat any Democratic nominee in the general election, especially a newcomer.

As a final blow, the mapmakers carved the Austin neighborhood where Doggett lived out of his district. He and his family moved to a different part of town so he could live in the district he hoped to represent.

Despite his opponents' efforts, Doggett won the next election. He also won the three after that, even though he was assigned to a new district where the lines hooked and sliced in different directions and contained different constituents.

Another round of redistricting followed the 2010 US census, and Republicans again tried to configure one in which Doggett would be absolutely sure to lose. The lines were drawn so that the population of his district was heavily made up of Hispanics living in San Antonio. These constituents, his opponents hoped, would vote for a local fellow Hispanic candidate rather than an Anglo from up in Austin.

In 2012, the US Supreme Court declared this map and several others in the state illegal because they discriminated against minorities. Once more Doggett's district was redrawn. This district was dubbed both the second most "squiggly" one in Texas and "the Upside-Down Elephant" because of an elongated appendage. In addition, his house ended up three blocks outside this newest district. The Constitution doesn't require representatives to live in their district. Tired of hopscotching, Doggett decided to stay put, meaning that he could no longer vote for himself.

LLOYD DOGGETT'S DISTRICTS 1995-2017

10TH
CONGRESSIONAL
DISTRICT

1995 – 2002
2003 – 2004

SAN ANTONIO

AUSTIN

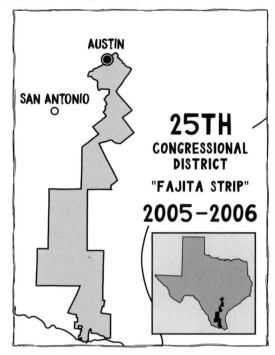

25TH
CONGRESSIONAL
DISTRICT

"FAJITA STRIP"

2005–2006

AUSTIN

SAN ANTONIO

AUSTIN

SAN ANTONIO

25TH
CONGRESSIONAL
DISTRICT

2007–2012

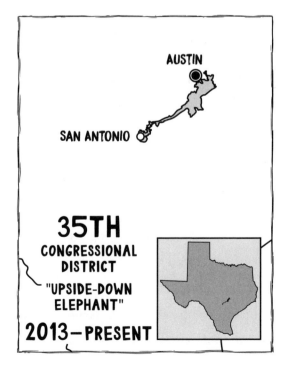

AUSTIN

SAN ANTONIO

35TH
CONGRESSIONAL
DISTRICT

"UPSIDE-DOWN
ELEPHANT"

2013–PRESENT

MISCHIEVOUS MAPMAKERS:
PACKING AND CRACKING

People who design congressional maps can use computer software that allows them to obtain certain outcomes for various district shapes and sizes. These include not only the number of people within a district but also the electorate's race, ethnicity, income level, and political party membership.

They can use this information to gerrymander—that is, manipulate—a district's boundaries to favor one party through several methods.

"Packing" refers to drawing district boundaries so that people who belong to a particular political party are grouped together in as few areas as possible. If they were represented in several districts, they could vote for—and possibly elect—many representatives. Packed together, they don't have as much influence in Congress.

"Cracking" takes the opposite approach. In this system of setting boundaries, members of a particular party are spread out so that they're in multiple districts but always in the political minority. This way, the person they vote for will lose every time.

Regular citizens can try out software, including *www.districtbuilder.org*, an online program, to come up with hypothetical alternative maps. You can also see how your district or any other one in the country has changed shape over time at *what-the-district.aclu.org*.

Meanwhile, Back in 1787 (and 1842)...

To create something (a government) out of practically nothing (the Articles of Confederation), the Framers faced a bewildering array of issues. They dispatched some of them in short order, barely anticipating the possible consequences.

Within days of convening in Philadelphia, the Framers agreed on a bicameral legislature and decided that the number of members each state could send to the House of Representatives would depend on the number of persons who lived in that state. The higher the population, the more representatives.

Setting up the basics of the government was the easy part. It then took them until the middle of July to define "persons."

ᔥ ᔣ

"Representatives and direct Taxes shall be apportioned among the several States which may be included within this Union, according to their respective Numbers, which shall be determined by adding to the whole Number of free Persons, including those bound to Service for a Term of Years, and excluding Indians not taxed, three fifths of all other Persons."

—Article I, Section 2

ᔥ ᔣ

Slavery was "the curse of heaven on the States where it prevailed."

—Gouverneur Morris, Pennsylvania

WHO COUNTS?

The Constitution makes clear that residents were not meant to be counted equally—and some not at all. "Indians" who did not pay taxes—meaning almost all Native Americans—were not included. Enslaved people, referred to as "other persons," were counted as only three-fifths of their total number. That is, one hundred enslaved persons were the equivalent of sixty free persons, and none of them could vote.

This mathematical formula came about because of a compromise. Framers from slaveholding states would have been delighted if each enslaved person counted as a whole person, so long as they had no right to vote. This way, those states would receive more representatives in Congress. Antislavery northerners, on the other hand, argued that enslaved people should not be counted at all. The Framers reluctantly agreed on what is now called the Three-Fifths Compromise proposed by James Wilson of Pennsylvania.

"South Carolina and Georgia cannot do without slaves."

—Charles Pinckney, South Carolina

◈ ◈

The Framers had no clue how many persons lived in the various states, let alone in the whole country. As a result, they didn't know what the size of the lower house would be. Estimates ranged from fifty-five to sixty-five members.

To verify the number of inhabitants, the Framers required that the national government hold a census every ten years, beginning in 1790. For the first census, federal marshals called "enumerators" hacked through roadless forests and forded bridgeless rivers to try to count each resident. Answer: 3.9 million persons, about 700,000 of whom were enslaved.

◈ ◈

"The actual Enumeration shall be made within three Years after the first Meeting of the Congress of the United States, and within every subsequent Term of ten Years, in such Manner as they shall by Law direct. The Number of Representatives shall not exceed one for every thirty Thousand, but each State shall have at Least one Representative…"

—Article I, Section 2

◈ ◈

With the basics in place, the Framers had to decide when, where, and how the people's representatives would be elected to office. Some Framers didn't trust the states to be in charge of elections. One especially suspicious group warned that if it were up to the states, some might never get around to holding elections.

Others had qualms about Congress making these decisions about the election process. Luther Martin of Maryland claimed that turning elections over to Congress was "designed for the utter extinction and abolition of all State governments."

HOW MANY REPRESENTATIVES?

Early drafts of the Constitution directed that there should be one member of Congress for every forty thousand citizens. James Madison of Virginia predicted that "if the union should be permanent, the number of representatives [would be] excessive." He changed the language so there would be not more than one representative for every forty thousand people. On the final day of the Convention, George Washington spoke up for the first time and reduced the number to thirty thousand because he knew the populace would object to the larger number.

That was fortunate because the US population is more than eighty times larger now than it was in 1787, and there are almost four times as many states. Had the original language remained in the Constitution, the House of Representatives would have nearly eleven thousand members today!

Yet, the House has not been expanded since 1911, when Congress set its size at 435 members. The country then held fewer than one-third the number of the people as it does now. The average district contains more than 750,000 inhabitants, and many Americans feel unheard by their representative. Montana's lone congressperson speaks for about a million constituents. For not many more people, Rhode Island gets two representatives.

James Wilson added that if Congress made the rules, it could require every voter in Pennsylvania, say, to show up in Philadelphia to cast their ballots. In that case, hardworking farmers who couldn't trek to the big cities would never get to vote.

In the end, most of the Framers didn't want to get into arguments about how, exactly, this new Congress they were creating should run elections. So, with no guidelines, they turned responsibility for planning and holding elections over to the states. In case the union did manage to last, they gave Congress the right to pass laws in the future to regulate elections.

༄ ༄

"The Times, Places and Manner of holding Elections for Senators and Representatives, shall be prescribed in each State by the Legislature thereof; but the Congress may at any time by Law make or alter such Regulations, except as the Places of chusing Senators."

—Article I, Section 4

༄ ༄

In 1842, Congress took advantage of its ability to control the elections of its members by adopting an Apportionment Act. The law requires every state to divide itself into single-member districts. However, Hawaii and New Mexico disobeyed the law until Congress reinforced it in 1967.

Nowadays we take it for granted that each member of the House comes from a single district and represents only that district. Before the Apportionment Act, though, some states elected all of their congressmen at-large, meaning from across the entire state. In such a system,

THE US CENSUS DOES MORE THAN COUNT NOSES

The decennial (every ten years) census continues to be controversial. Information about income and race are important for planning congressional districts and government programs. Yet some people don't want to tell census-takers how much they earn. Others identify with more than one race. Americans living abroad, such as Mormons doing missionary work, aren't counted at all—possibly costing Utah a representative in the House.

The Trump administration proposed asking everyone in 2020 if they're citizens, causing undocumented immigrants to fear that they'll be discovered and deported. L awsuits over this issue headed to the Supreme Court. Other recent wrinkles are that Congress hasn't allocated enough money to test new census-taking software, and the Bureau didn't have a permanent director from 2017 to 2019. Many people, including former census directors, worry the 2020 census will be unreliable.

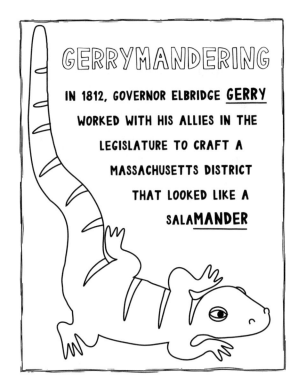

GERRYMANDERING

IN 1812, GOVERNOR ELBRIDGE **GERRY** WORKED WITH HIS ALLIES IN THE LEGISLATURE TO CRAFT A MASSACHUSETTS DISTRICT THAT LOOKED LIKE A SALA<u>MANDER</u>

later, though, that it has created its own problems, including opportunities for hijinks by state legislators when they draw congressional boundaries.

So What's the Big Problem?

Usually we think of elections as opportunities for voters to pick their leaders. But when politicians have the power to shift district boundary lines around to suit themselves, they can preselect the voters who will put them into office. (Senators can't use these tactics because they represent the entire state.)

America has a long history of such shenanigans. In 1788, Patrick Henry tried to keep James Madison out of the House of Representatives by creating a cockeyed district for him. Although Henry failed, attempts to skew districts have continued ever since.

The results of Texas's ongoing gerrymandering has the potential to affect the rest of the country. Here's why. Texas sends the country's second highest number of representatives to

people whose views are in the minority can be frozen out entirely. Only the opinions of the majority, even if it's narrow, get represented in Congress.

With single-member districts, some could be composed of residents who hold different views from those in other districts. They would then have a better chance of electing someone who agreed with them.

That did solve the problem facing Congress in 1842. We can see 175 years

Washington. So even if a majority of the country voted for the Democratic party, Texas alone could possibly help Republicans keep control of Congress.

❧ ❧

"...this is the most aggressive map I have ever seen. This has a real national impact that should assure that Republicans keep the House no matter the national mood."

—Joby Fortson, a member of the staff of Texas Republican Congressman Joe Barton

❧ ❧

After the 2010 census, Republicans developed a plan to win over as many state legislatures as possible. Called Redistricting the Majority Project (REDMAP) the strategy succeeded; the majority of both houses of the legislatures in twenty-five states changed from Democratic blue to Republican red. These chambers then redrew their states' congressional maps to favor Republican candidates. Then, in the 2012 House election, although Democrats across the country snagged nearly 1.4

REDMAP WAS ESPECIALLY SUCCESSFUL IN 2018

IN OHIO, DEMOCRATS WON 45% OF THE VOTE BUT REPUBLICANS GOT 75% OF HOUSE SEATS — 45% / 75%

IN TEXAS, THE TWO PARTIES GOT ABOUT THE SAME NUMBER OF VOTES BUT REPUBLICANS GOT 64% OF THE HOUSE SEATS — 50% 50% / 64%

IN NORTH CAROLINA, THE PARTIES ALSO SPLIT THE VOTE BUT REPUBLICANS GOT 69% OF HOUSE SEATS — 50% 50% / 69%

million more votes, Republicans captured thirty-three more seats. A website called Puzzling Shapes shows how they handled Doggett's district.

Democrats have also created district maps that skew electoral results. Federal judges in Illinois labeled the maps Democrats crafted after the 2010 census "a blatant political move to increase the number of Democratic congressional seats." The outline of a district in Maryland that was drawn by

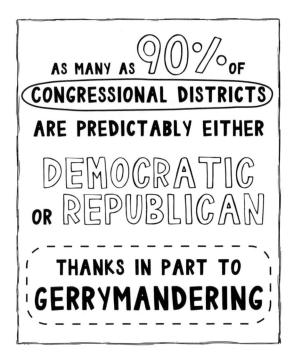

AS MANY AS 90% OF CONGRESSIONAL DISTRICTS ARE PREDICTABLY EITHER DEMOCRATIC OR REPUBLICAN THANKS IN PART TO GERRYMANDERING

Democrats is so scattershot, it's been described as looking like "blood spatter from a crime scene." The governor, Democrat Martin O'Malley, even admitted to a judge that he intended to keep his party in power. The result is that Maryland sent seven Democrats and only one Republican to the House of Representatives after the 2018 election. And New Jersey, which elected just one Republican congressperson out of twelve, is even more skewed. Still, because Republicans captured many state legislatures in 2010, gerrymanders

favored them overall until at least 2020.

In response to REDMAP and the results of the 2016 election, former-President Barack Obama and his Attorney General Eric Holder set up the National Democratic Redistricting Committee (NRDC). They planned to develop a "strategy that shifts the redistricting power, creating fair districts where Democrats can compete."

Across the country, Democratic candidates for the House won about 53 percent of the vote and about the same percentage of the seats in 2018. It's possible that map drawing based on an eight-year-old census is less precise, as people move in and out of established districts and population size becomes unequal.

Still, gerrymandering for political and racial reasons persists. When politicians know that members of their own party control their chances of winning the next election, they have little incentive to compromise with members of the opposition party. If they do compromise, angry members of their own party might challenge them in a primary, and their constituents might switch their support to the challenger.

An unwillingness to compromise can lead to gridlock. This is especially the case when we have a divided government—that is, when different parties are in charge of Congress and the White House.

If one party gains control of both houses and the presidency, gridlock can be broken, assuming the party is united. Lawmakers can pass legislation, confident that the president will sign it. However, a gerrymandered lower house and an upper house with two senators for every state might not represent the will of the people. A majority of the electorate might be furious about those very laws.

There Are Other Ways
States
Several states, including Arizona, California, and Idaho, have taken the power to draw congressional district lines away from elected state officials.

THE **US** RANKED 52ND OUT OF 153 COUNTRIES

IN A 2012-2014 SURVEY OF THE INTEGRITY OF ELECTION SYSTEMS AROUND THE WORLD

WHAT WAS THE GREATEST PROBLEM? PARTISAN INFLUENCE IN ELECTORAL PROCEDURES

Instead, citizen commissions that have little connection to any political party create the maps. This movement is gaining traction. In 2018, Colorado, Michigan, Missouri, and Ohio overwhelmingly passed ballot measures to put redistricting in the hands of nonpartisan groups. Utah did so by a bare majority. And, Virginia is considering a constitutional amendment requiring an independent commission.

In the meantime, though, Michigan and Ohio held elections in the districts that had been drawn after the 2010 census. In 2019, courts declared these districts to be unconstitutional, because they were gerrymandered for partisan purposes, and demanded that new districts be drawn in time for the 2020 election.

Iowa turns the task over to an independent, nonpartisan commission that does not consider the party affiliations of voters. Their charge is to devise districts that are compact, equal in size, and a mix of rural and urban locales. Iowa's system has been called "a model of equity—and a model for the nation." Races that used to be predictable are up for grabs, so candidates have to pay attention to a wider array of their constituents' opinions.

Some state legislatures are required to follow such rules when they devise districts. In Florida, for example, mapmakers must make districts as compact as

REDISTRICTING EVEN HELPS COUNTIES

In 2017, a federal judge ordered officials in San Juan County, Utah, to redraw district lines so that members of the Navajo Nation, who make up a majority of the local population, would have a shot at winning seats on the county commission. In a 2018 special election, two Native American men won.

possible and must not divide up communities, as happened in Austin. But requirements for compact districts can backfire, since people who live in the same neighborhood often hold similar opinions, creating packed districts.

Other Countries

Some foreign countries that continue to use single-member districts rely on nonpartisan commissions similar to those in Arizona, California, and Idaho to draw political boundaries. They include Albania, Australia, the Bahamas, Barbados, Botswana, Britain, Canada, Germany, New Zealand, and Zimbabwe.

But most countries have moved away from a system that relies solely upon single-member districts as the United States does. Germany and New Zealand, for example, elect half of their parliament from single-member districts; the other half is elected in a nationwide vote. The ultimate allocation of seats takes into account the overall national percentages. So gerrymandering is not a problem there.

Countries with multimember districts are finding that candidates are more diverse. Also, they don't need to redraw boundary lines, even if the population of a district changes, because the number of representatives elected from the district can easily be increased or decreased in proportion to shifts in the population.

The United States

The Constitution gives Congress the power to pass laws about the electoral process. Therefore, Congress could mandate a number of fixes to the problem of gerrymandering.

Congress could require that nonpartisan commissions plan districts in every state. Or it could mandate that states follow national standards and requirements. This way, election procedures would be consistent across the country.

Perhaps the most important proposal would repeal the 1842 Apportionment Act requiring single-member districts. Congress could then pass a new law directing states with large enough populations to elect their representatives from multimember districts using proportional representation.

For example, Texas, which sends thirty-six representatives to Congress, could be divided into six large districts, each of which would elect six representatives. If they were chosen by proportional representation, it is practically guaranteed that minority viewpoints would not be shut out. Under this scheme, the half-million Republicans in New York City who lost their only Republican member of Congress in the 2018 election would be represented by someone more to their liking. So would the third of the people in Arkansas who are Democrats.

What about the size of the House of Representatives? Legislatures in most modern democracies have about as many members as the cube root of their country's population. The cube root of 326 million is 688. With 100 senators, that means a House of 588 representatives—a manageable increase.

The Story Continues

Doggett must be either a lucky or very effective politician. Despite living outside his own district, he kept his seat in Congress not only in the 2012 election but also through the next three. Hard as they tried, Republican mapmakers did not succeed in ousting him. But gerrymandering often works, and the

Republicans prevailed in another way.

Austin is the capital of Texas and the eleventh largest city in the country. It is also the biggest city that is not represented by a single congressperson in Congress. Instead, it is sliced and diced into five districts that meander far from town. Though a majority of the populace leans strongly Democratic, four of its five representatives are Republicans.

In 2017, a federal court declared that eleven of the state's district maps, including Doggett's district, purposely discriminated against Hispanic and black voters. The Supreme Court disagreed and ruled that only one district—not Doggett's—needed to be redrawn. Even gerrymandered, that one remained unchanged until the 2020 election.

CHAPTER 6

Taxation without Representation
The District of Columbia

"Free DC!"

On April 11, 2011, District of Columbia Mayor Vincent Gray joined a group of about two hundred protesters chanting "Free DC!" and "We can't take it anymore!" outside the Hart Senate Office Building on Constitution Avenue. The mayor, along with half a dozen members of the district's city council, sat down in the middle of the street in front of a banner that read, "Washington, DC. No Taxation Without Representation."

As Gray had expected, he was arrested by Capitol Police, along with about forty other protesters, for "unlawful assembly" and "blocking passage." Gray told reporters he was "fighting for the freedom of the people of the District of Columbia."

The mayor was referring to the right of DC residents to determine how the taxes they pay to the city should be spent and how the town they live in should be governed. Even though the citizenry paid local taxes amounting to $5.5 billion that year, these decisions were out of their control.

Several months earlier, the city council had decided to use city tax revenue to pay for programs that provided abortion services for low-income women. In response, Congress passed a bill that barred the city from spending its funds in this way. Congress's power to prevent DC from using its own money however the council saw fit was the reason the mayor joined the protest.

۽ ۾

"All we want to do is spend
our own money."

—Mayor Vincent Gray, DC

۽ ۾

Meanwhile, Back in 1787 (and 1890, 1961, 1973, 1978, and 2013)...

The location of the national capital was uncertain. After Revolutionary War soldiers stormed Congress's headquarters in Philadelphia in 1783, demanding their unpaid wages, officials fled to Princeton, New Jersey. Four months later, they picked up and moved to Annapolis, Maryland, then to a tavern in Trenton, New Jersey, and, in January 1785, to New York City. There, George Washington took his first oath of office in 1789.

Many New Yorkers thought it would be a fine idea for their hometown to continue to serve as the capital city. But those who did not live in New York were suspicious; they did not want that state to dominate the new federal government.

The Framers decided that the national capital needed to be located in a special area, not connected to any particular state. But where?

The solution resulted from a deal between Virginians Thomas Jefferson and James Madison on one side and New Yorker Alexander Hamilton on the other. The three kept the negotiations secret, and no one else was in the room. But the Compromise of 1790 involved a trade: Jefferson and Madison would support Hamilton's proposal that the national government pay off the states' war debts, including money owed to the impoverished veterans of the Revolution. In return, the new "federal town," as they called the capital, would be established along the Potomac River on land donated by Maryland and Virginia—but belonging to no state. Instead, with Congress as the reason for the town's existence, it made sense that this body would oversee the town.

∾ ∾

"The Congress shall have Power To... exercise exclusive Legislation in all Cases whatsoever, over such District (not exceeding ten Miles square) as may, by Cession of particular States, and the Acceptance of Congress, become the Seat of the Government of the United States..."

—Article I, Section 8

∾ ∾

John Adams, the second president, became the first to live in Washington, the District of Columbia. Since then, its citizens' attempts to gain a voice in Congress have mostly been muffled.

In 1890, Senator Henry Blair, a Republican, proposed an amendment to give the District representation in the House and Senate without DC's being designated a state. It was ignored. The District came closest to congressional representation in 1978, when a similar amendment passed both houses and had the support of President Jimmy Carter. But only sixteen states approved it before the seven years allotted for ratification ran out. A debate about the issue in 1993 ended when Congressman John Dingell, a Democrat from Michigan, said that if DC residents are unhappy with the situation, "They can leave anytime they want."

The unhappy citizenry tried again in 2013 when a bill was introduced to admit the state of New Columbia into the union. The measure was sent to the Committee on Homeland Security and Governmental Affairs and hasn't been heard of since.

Meantime, the District won two meaningful but partial victories. The Twenty-third Amendment, ratified in 1961, finally allowed US citizens who live in DC to vote in presidential elections. Some of these people worked for the president! And, beginning in 1973, they could at last have their own mayor and city council.

So What's the Big Problem?

The District of Columbia is really a territory—though it's called a city—

RESIDENTS OF DC DEAL WITH AN ONGOING SERIES OF INSULTS AND BARRIERS

- Congress can pass just about any law it decides to impose on the District.
- Congress also reviews every law passed by the DC Council before it can take effect, delaying statutes needed to help residents.
- Inhabitants pay more per person in federal income taxes than the residents of any state.
- The District raises billions of dollars in local taxes every year but cannot spend the money unless Congress allows it to by passing a law.
- Members of the military from the District risk their lives to establish democratic systems abroad but cannot participate in their own nation's system by electing a voting representative in Congress when they return home.
- In 2014, voters approved an ordinance allowing residents to grow and possess small amounts of marijuana in private homes in the District. Congress then passed a law preventing the city from taxing sales of the substance. This was a hardship, since the city council had hoped to use the funds to update schools and bridges.
- Trash wasn't picked up in DC for more than three weeks during the 1995–96 federal government shutdowns over budget disagreements in Congress.
- During the 2019 shutdown, the District picked up the federal government's trash and provided water to government buildings, without being paid.
- Every state is allowed to display two statues in the US Capitol building. The District does not have that right.

rather than a state, and DC isn't even *in* a state. More people live in the District than in either Wyoming or Vermont. Each of these states sends one representative and two senators to Congress. The District sends zero. They can only send a nonvoting delegate to the House of Representatives. She can speak—but that's all. DCers, most of whom are racial or ethnic minorities, have no role in making the nation's laws, including how much federal tax they pay.

DC residents elect a mayor and city council just as residents of most other cities do. However, Congress holds the

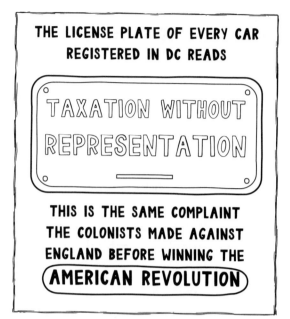

THE LICENSE PLATE OF EVERY CAR REGISTERED IN DC READS

TAXATION WITHOUT REPRESENTATION

THIS IS THE SAME COMPLAINT THE COLONISTS MADE AGAINST ENGLAND BEFORE WINNING THE AMERICAN REVOLUTION

North Carolina and Alabama filed bills in 2018 that would prevent the District from spending its own money to implement its own laws.

Because the 700,000 citizens of DC are not represented by a voting member in Congress, they can't even effectively complain about this state of affairs. The District is the only capital in the democratic world without a vote in the national legislature or full home rule.

power to overturn every law the council adopts and every action taken by its mayor. Furthermore, the city requires that people who work for the local government to live in DC—where they cannot vote in federal elections.

On top of that, Congress has ultimate control over the District's budget. Local politicians have to hope that the federal government will let them spend their own money as they see fit without meddling. As the maddening events that led to Gray's protest illustrate, that's not always the case. This situation could get worse since members of Congress from

℘ ℘

"Although I was proud to see the Iraqis exercise their right to vote for...representation in their new democracy, I could not vote for such a representative...in our country."

—Captain Yolanda Lee, DC resident who served in Iraq in 2005, when that country held its first elections in 50 years

℘ ℘

In 2009, leaders in the Senate demanded that the District roll back its restrictions on possession of firearms in order to get approval for a voting representative in the House. DC refused. Nonvoting Congresswoman Eleanor Holmes Norton called the dilemma "heartbreaking."

There Are Other Ways
Other Countries

The capital cities of several other countries are not part of a state. These include Brasilia in Brazil, Buenos Aires in Argentina, Canberra in Australia, Delhi in India, and Mexico City in Mexico.

But no country other than the United States prevents its capital city from being represented in its legislature. Argentina, Australia, Brazil, India, Mexico, and Venezuela used to do so but have eliminated those restrictions.

Canberra, the capital of Australia, has only one delegate to the house and two senators to the upper house (rather than the twelve assigned to each of the six Australian states). Still, citizens of the capital are not voiceless as those in DC are.

The United States

There is no doubt that DC residents want a voice in Congress. Nearly 86 percent of voters supported a referendum on statehood in 2016. A state constitution was drafted in which the mayor would become governor; the city council would become a unicameral; and local citizens could choose their members of Congress.

❧ ❧

"Statehood remains a nonstarter… You're not going to find Republicans willing to just give Democrats two Senate seats."
—Congressman Tom Davis, Virginia

❧ ❧

Even if the District isn't entitled to two senators because it's not a state, most of its citizens would like to be represented by at least a voting member of the House. Making that change would probably require a constitutional amendment.

Another possibility would be to shrink the district boundaries to just the area where the national government buildings—the Capitol, the White House, and federal agencies—are located. Residential neighborhoods would be returned to Virginia and Maryland, and residents would be represented in Congress. These two states would have to agree to accept them, of course. This proposal is called retrocession, and it's not a new idea.

In 1847, Congress agreed to retrocede—or give back—to Virginia the areas where the cities of Arlington and Alexandria sit today. The federal government was smaller then and didn't need the land. Furthermore, that part of the state had become a major center of the slave trade. Fearful that Congress would abolish the selling of enslaved people in the District—as it did in 1850—the state took back about thirty square miles.

The Story Continues

Gray and his fellow protesters spent seven hours in jail before being released. The District has yet to acquire either voting representation or statehood; however, Democrats in both the House and the Senate introduced legislation in 2019 to make DC the fifty-first state.

WHAT ABOUT PUERTO RICO?

The United States includes five territories whose status, like that of Washington, DC, is irregular. Two—Puerto Rico and the US Virgin Islands—are in the Caribbean. The other three—American Samoa, Guam, and the Northern Mariana Islands—are in the mid-Pacific Ocean.

Most residents on these islands are American citizens, except for American Samoans, who have the status of "US nationals." Unlike Washingtonians, however, they cannot vote for president. Like the residents of DC, they have only a nonvoting representative, called a delegate, in the House. The Constitution gives Congress the right to admit territories to the union but doesn't lay out any criteria for membership.

Puerto Rico, which has a population of about 3.7 million people, is the largest of these territories in both area and population. Understandably, Puerto Ricans have a variety of views about how they're governed. In 2012, opinion was evenly split between those who wanted their island to become a full-fledged state and those who supported the current arrangement; a small percentage favored establishing a separate country. Five years later, 97 percent of those who voted supported statehood; however, most voters sat out the election, possibly because they don't.

Later that year, Hurricane Maria devastated Puerto Rico, killing thousands of people. The island's delegate to Congress filed a bill, which was cosponsored by thirty-five members of the House, that would make it a state by 2021. Meanwhile, the territory declared a form of bankruptcy, and its finances are supervised by a board on the mainland.

CHAPTER 7

"I'll Just Do It Myself!" "Oh No You Won't."
Direct Democracy

Go Blue!

When Jennifer Gratz applied to college in 1995, she was pretty confident she'd be admitted to the prestigious University of Michigan. She held a 3.8 grade point average in high school and was active in a number of extracurricular activities. Her heart was set on attending U of M's flagship campus in Ann Arbor.

Although the university admitted her, Gratz was disappointed to learn she was shunted to the less appealing campus in Dearborn. She later learned that, in making its decisions, the admissions office awarded extra points to minority applicants, among others. Following a policy called affirmative action, officials wanted to be sure that the university would enroll a diverse range of students.

But as a white student, Gratz felt discriminated against. Why should she be rejected in favor of someone with a lower GPA? Offended by the university's policy, she took action.

In 2003, she sued the university in a case that reached the Supreme Court—and won. But a similar case decided the same day upheld a slightly different version of affirmative action at the U of M Law School. Believing that affirmative action is inappropriate everywhere and in all cases, Gratz proposed an amendment to the state constitution to eliminate it.

Michigan allows ordinary citizens

to propose state constitutional amendments if they can show there is widespread support for change. Following the process—and with help from organizations that, like her, opposed affirmative action—Gratz collected over 320,000 signatures on a petition. This was more than enough to meet the requirement for her proposed amendment to be voted on in a state-wide election.

When Proposal 2 came up for a vote in 2006, 58 percent of the voters approved. The new section in the state constitution banned "public institutions from using affirmative action programs that give preferential treatment to groups or individuals based on their race, gender, color, ethnicity or national origin…" Gratz, a private, unelected citizen, succeeded in changing her state's constitution by direct action.

Meanwhile, Back in 1787…

The Framers never imagined that citizens would ever directly make laws or revise the Constitution on their own initiative. James Madison of Virginia explained that the basis of the Constitution is its "total exclusion of the people, in their collective capacity, from any share" in actually governing. Only the people's representatives—not the people themselves—would be able to make actual decisions about public policies.

So What's the Big Problem?

Although our Constitution was written in the name of "We the People," the people themselves have no explicit power at the national level. Our government relies entirely on 535 representatives and senators (plus the president, the cabinet, judges, and, especially these days, administrative agencies) to make laws and rules for us.

We can try to influence the laws, regulations, and policies through letter-writing campaigns, protests, social media, news editorials, financial contributions to candidates, lobbying, testifying before Congress, and other means. But multiple obstacles block the way. We can't actually create or revise national laws the way Gratz did in the state of Michigan. Direct democracy offers an end run around the barriers.

There Are Other Ways

States

Almost all states allow for some form of direct democracy as well as representative government. Instead of relying solely on elected officials, citizens can take actions into their own hands. Since 1900, nearly fourteen thousand proposed measures have gone directly to voters! Nebraska's unicameral came about when a citizen initiative and referendum abolished the state senate. States allow voters to make their voices heard through proposing amendments and legislation in a variety of ways.

Every state except Delaware requires that a majority of voters approve proposed state constitutional amendments before they can take effect. In Delaware, the state legislature can amend the constitution without any involvement by the people.

Many western states, including Arizona, California, and Oregon, allow the electorate to put proposals, including state constitutional amendments, on the ballot. Then a statewide vote determines whether they should be adopted.

Maine and Ohio allow the electorate to challenge laws passed by the state legislature. If enough voters sign petitions, the challenged laws are voted on at the next election.

In fourteen states, the electorate gets to decide every ten or twenty years or so whether to hold a state constitutional convention. If a majority calls for one, the citizenry has the opportunity to cure the defects in the existing constitution. New Hampshire has had seventeen such conventions since 1789! Some states choose to replace their existing constitutions with a brand-new one during a constitutional convention and then must get approval from the electorate.

This form of direct democracy has become so popular, however, that elected state officials are balking at abiding by voters' wishes. In 2016, legislatures refused to accept the results of one-quarter of the initiatives passed across the country. Maine Governor Paul LePage said they are "pure democracy, and it has not worked for 15,000 years." He might be wrong. In 2018, voters in at least fourteen states passed more than nineteen referenda on such major issues as abortion policy, minimum wage and legalizing marijuana.

Other Countries

Referenda—votes on specific issues by the electorate—are increasingly common around the world. Switzerland is especially known for using them. Other countries that make frequent use of referenda include Australia and New Zealand.

Out of 174 countries, 141 have held at least one national referendum since 1980. Only thirty-three countries, including the United States, have not held one, and many of them are repressive regimes like Afghanistan and Cuba.

Sometimes a national referendum gets international attention. In 2015, Ireland, a largely Catholic country, voted by a large majority to legalize same-sex marriage in a national referendum. In 2016, a different referendum in Britain led that country to decide to leave the European Union.

The United States

Perhaps citizens should be able to side-step Congress and pass or erase certain laws on their own. This process exists in a number of states, so why not at the national level? Perhaps it would be a good idea to amend the Constitution to give citizens not only a voice that they lack within "representative government" but also an important way of participating in government itself.

The Story Continues

Opponents challenged the constitutionality of Jennifer Gratz's amendment in federal court but the US Supreme Court upheld it in 2014 by a vote of 6 to 2.

PART III
If America Threw a Party, Would You Be Let In?

Self-government relies on citizens being able to choose their leaders, generally through elections. But the Constitution doesn't guarantee that all citizens actually have the right to vote. Nor does the Constitution make it easy for citizens to run for certain offices.

In this section, we show you how

- states can control citizens' access to the polls, depending on whether they want to decrease or increase the number of voters;
- the Constitution makes it impossible for some otherwise eligible candidates to run for public office; and
- a president can't necessarily finish the job he was elected to do.

In the first case, the percentage of citizens who get to vote or who can do so easily varies widely from state to state. In the second, voters lose the opportunity to choose leaders whom they might like but who can't run because of restrictions in the Constitution. One of these restrictions applies to the president, the highest executive in the land.

CHAPTER 8

Who Can Vote? How Do You Know?
Voting Rights

"If I Had a Concealed Handgun Permit"

In June 2015, Mary Lou Miller, age 101, tried to vote in the election for the mayor of San Antonio, Texas. She had been voting regularly in almost every election since she turned twenty-one, only fourteen years after the Nineteenth Amendment gave women the ballot in 1920. Believing it was important to be involved in politics, she had taught classes about the candidates and issues, registered voters, and driven them to the polls. But this time, she was deprived of the chance to cast her own ballot.

Texas state law allows certain groups of people to vote by mail. To be eligible, applicants must be at least sixty-five years old, disabled, out of town, or in jail. Miller met the first requirement and applied for a mail-in ballot, as she had in the past. But she had recently moved from one home for senior citizens to another, and the post office doesn't forward ballots. As a result, she didn't receive hers.

So she went to her precinct to vote early in person, since registered voters can cast their ballots several weeks before Election Day. However, at this point, the law turned against her.

Only people who could produce a government-issued proof of identity with a photograph, such as a driver's license or passport, were able to vote at the polls. Miller did not have one. She was barred from voting early and was directed to the Texas Department of Public Safety (DPS) to obtain an approved form of ID. Fortunately, she had a few days before voting ended.

But things got complicated at DPS. To prove that she was really Mary Lou Miller, she needed to supply one of the following primary documents:

- a driver's license—but she hadn't driven in over twenty years and had let it lapse
- a passport—but since she didn't travel abroad, she didn't have one
- a military ID—but she'd never enlisted
- a parole document—but she'd never been jailed

In place of these, she could provide a combination of other documents, none of which she owned. Here is Miller's own explanation of the situation:

"I could produce either two documents from the secondary identification documents list or one from the secondary list plus two from the supporting identification documents. Sorry, but I have never seen my birth certificate, if, indeed, one was issued. I was born in Luxor, a very tiny unincorporated coal village in Southwestern Pennsylvania, and maybe they recorded my birth, but I don't have a copy. Nor was I born abroad, and I don't possess a certified copy of a court order indicating a change of name.

"I do have some supporting identification documents like my Medicare and Social Security cards and the voter registration card at the old address, but without a secondary identification document, I am simply out of luck. Even if I had a concealed handgun permit or a pilot's license, lacking a certified birth certificate makes it impossible to get the photo ID, thereby making it impossible for me to vote early in-person or on Election Day."

৩ ৶

"My vote won't count... Vote for those of us who cannot."

—Mary Lou Miller

৩ ৶

Meanwhile, Back in 1787 (and 1868, 1870, 1920, 1964, and 1971)…

The Framers did not address the subject of who had the right to vote. They assumed that there would be elections and voters, but who could vote and how was left up to the states, even if they each concocted entirely different procedures.

ॐ ॐ

"The House of Representatives shall be composed of Members chosen every second Year by the People of the several States, and the Electors in each State shall have the Qualifications requisite for Electors of the most numerous Branch of the State Legislature."

—Article I, Section 2

ॐ ॐ

Not surprisingly, every state did come up with its own rules.

In most states, only men could vote. New Jersey alone allowed women to do so—but only wealthy, unmarried women. That's because only people worth at least fifty pounds had the right to vote, and, when a woman married, her property went to her husband. In 1807, New Jersey women lost the right to vote as the result of a dispute between the major political parties.

Some states required that voters own property or pay taxes.

All states limited suffrage—the right to vote—to persons over the age of twenty-one, the age of adulthood.

No state allowed enslaved people to vote. But some allowed free blacks to do so, while others did not.

Some of these restrictions were barred following the Civil War. In 1870, five years after Confederate General Robert E. Lee surrendered to Union General Ulysses S. Grant at Appomattox, the reunited nation adopted the Fifteenth Amendment. This prohibits states from making it hard or impossible for people to vote because of their race.

ॐ ॐ

"The right of citizens of the United States to vote shall not be denied or

95

abridged by the United States or by any State on account of race, color, or previous condition of servitude. The Congress shall have power to enforce this article by appropriate legislation."

—Fifteenth Amendment

ᔕ ᔕ

Officials in some states then required that voters pass difficult literacy tests or pay poll taxes. Although they claimed these laws were not racist, many African Americans were still denied the right to vote.

Thereafter:

The women's suffrage movement had split over whether or not to support the Fifteenth Amendment. If men of any color could vote, why not women? Finally, fifty years later, in 1920, the Nineteenth Amendment allowed women to vote.

ᔕ ᔕ

"The right of citizens of the United States to vote shall not be denied or abridged by the United States or by any State on account of sex. Congress shall

have power to enforce this article by appropriate legislation."

—Nineteenth Amendment

ᔕ ᔕ

The Twenty-fourth Amendment, added in 1964, prevents states from charging "poll taxes" to vote in state elections for federal officials. Southern states, in particular, had used this tactic to make it harder for poor people to vote.

ᔕ ᔕ

"The right of citizens of the United States to vote in any primary or other election for President or Vice President, for electors for President or Vice President, or for Senator or Representative in Congress, shall not be denied or abridged by the United States or any State by reason of failure to pay any poll tax or other tax. The Congress shall have power to enforce this article by appropriate legislation."

—Twenty-fourth Amendment

ᔕ ᔕ

In 1971, the Twenty-sixth Amendment changed the age of adulthood from twenty-one to eighteen.

ଡ଼ ଈ

"The right of citizens of the United States, who are eighteen years of age or older, to vote shall not be denied or abridged by the United States or any state on account of age. The Congress shall have power to enforce this article by appropriate legislation."

—Twenty-sixth Amendment

ଡ଼ ଈ

More recently, voting-rights activists have used the Fourteenth Amendment, which was adopted in 1868, to try to prevent states from restricting the right to vote. This amendment guarantees all citizens "equal protection" under the law. For instance, they argue, requiring that people live in a state for more than a brief period of time before voting there makes them unequal with other residents.

ଡ଼ ଈ

"No State shall…deny to any person within its jurisdiction the equal protection of the laws."

—Fourteenth Amendment

ଡ଼ ଈ

It might appear that constitutional amendments have increased voters' access to the polls, no matter where they live. That's not entirely true.

So What's the Big Problem?

States are all over the map when it comes to voting laws. Their policies depend on how easy—or difficult—they want to make it for citizens to vote.

Sometimes the courts step in. For instance, in spring 2016, a federal court struck down three provisions in a North Carolina law. The law had stiffened voter ID requirements, reduced the number of early-voting days, and stopped allowing sixteen- and seventeen- year-olds to preregister to vote when they took driver's ed. On the other hand, in 2018, the Supreme Court allowed Ohio to purge people from the rolls if they had missed a few elections.

Texas, like many states, claims that people who are not eligible to vote may try to impersonate someone else at the polls. To prevent this crime, called voter fraud, they require an ID. Miller lost her right to vote because she didn't have one. Voter fraud does happen, though extremely rarely. President Donald J. Trump set up a Commission on Election Integrity to investigate the issue. Before it was disbanded, the members uncovered about a thousand possible cases of fraud out of a billion votes since the year 2000—that's a one in a million chance.

Fraud regarding absentee ballots in a House race in North Carolina in 2018 led the state's electoral commission to invalidate the results and call for a new election in September 2019. Meanwhile, the district was not represented in Congress.

Voting rules are not neutral. While some states are easing access to the polls, others are limiting it.

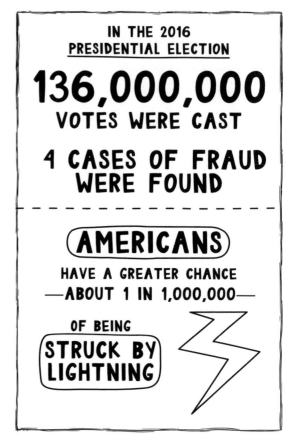

IN THE 2016 PRESIDENTIAL ELECTION

136,000,000 VOTES WERE CAST

4 CASES OF FRAUD WERE FOUND

AMERICANS HAVE A GREATER CHANCE —ABOUT 1 IN 1,000,000— OF BEING STRUCK BY LIGHTNING

Take a look at this hodgepodge of procedures and requirements, as of 2018.

Residence

• Some states refuse to count college students as residents or make it practically impossible for them to vote at school. Undergrads at Prairie View A&M University sued in 2018 when county officials told them to register using an address in the wrong precinct.

17 STATES
INTRODUCED (NEW) VOTER RESTRICTIONS IN TIME FOR THE 2016 PRESIDENTIAL ELECTION

• Twenty-six states require residence ranging from ten days to thirty days before registering to vote. The other twenty-four have no residence requirement.

Registration

• Since 2015, seventeen states, including Illinois, Massachusetts, and Rhode Island, plus the District of Columbia allow automatic voter registration (AVR) when people renew their driver's licenses or get IDs at a motor vehicle office.

• Seventeen states plus DC allow people to register when they show up at the polls on Election Day.

• Thirty-four states and DC allow online registration. The other states require people to appear in advance at official sites, sometimes inconveniently located, with documentation to prove their identity and eligibility.

• New Yorkers who want to change their political party affiliation must do so more than a year before the election. Ivanka Trump did not and was unable to vote for her father in the 2016 presidential primary.

• More than six million people across the country have lost the right to vote because of their criminal records. Only Maine and Vermont allow felons to vote while they're serving their sentences. Nebraska automatically restores voting rights to former felons (many of whom prefer to be called "returning citizens") two years after they're released; Wyoming does so for those who have committed nonviolent crimes. Floridians passed a referendum in 2018 that restored voting rights to nonviolent felons, though the legislature limited their eligibility. Many states, however, continue to bar felons from the polls forever, though governors in some states, including Arizona and Iowa, can decide to restore that right on a case-by-case basis.

Identification

• Nineteen states do not require identification during voter registration.

• Thirty-six states require that voters produce some form of identification at the polls:

◆ Of these, seventeen say the ID must include a photograph. This form of identification often costs money, making it expensive for low-income people to obtain. A federal court in Texas found that more than six hundred thousand registered voters could be turned away at the polls because they don't hold the state's required proof of ID.

◆ In some states, an ID can be a hunting license, an electric bill, a student identification card, or other options.

◆ Some states allow voters who arrive without ID to fill in a provisional ballot, which is counted only after they produce other documents; others don't allow this. When Georgia's Secretary of State, Brian Kemp, whose job was to oversee elections, ran for governor in 2018, he insisted that voters' IDs match their registrations exactly—no missing spaces or hyphens allowed. A federal judge ordered that they be allowed to use a provisional ballot.

Polling Hours

• Thirty-eight states plus the District of Columbia allow people to cast their ballots before Election Day, although the time period ranges from less than two weeks to over a month beforehand.

• Three states require that all ballots be mailed.

• The rest allow voting only on one day and only between certain limited hours, which vary from state to state.

Citizens' ability to register and vote continues to vary widely, depending on

BE SURE TO VOTE FOR YOUR SECOND CHOICE!

Voters usually check the box for one person in an election—the person they most want to win. But, when three or more candidates are on the ballot, the winner might not get a majority of the votes. There's another way to vote that helps make sure that the person favored by most voters wins. It's called Ranked-Choice or Instant-Runoff Voting.

Instead of marking one box, voters indicate their first, second, and third choices. If one gets a majority—game over. If no one does, then the candidate with the fewest first-choice votes drops out, and that person's vote is distributed to the second favorite. This process keeps going until a winner with a majority emerges.

It sounds complicated but the system works well in Australia, Ireland, and New Zealand as well as San Francisco and Minneapolis. A House candidate in Maine who came in first with less than 50 percent of the vote in 2018, however, sued to undo the reallocation of second-place votes, which tipped the victory to his opponent. He later dropped the suit.

where they live. Furthermore, registering and voting don't necessarily go hand in hand. A federal court in Texas found that more than 600,000 registered voters would be turned away at the polls because they don't hold the state's required proof of identification. This situation is likely to keep changing. As of 2018, legislators in forty-one states introduced a total of 514 bills to increase access to voting. At the same time, legislators in twenty-seven states did the opposite.

It turns out these regulations matter. States such as Minnesota that allow same-day voter registration have the highest turnout of voters. In 2016, nearly 75 percent of eligible Minnesotans voted!

There Are Other Ways
States

In 2016, Oregon led the way in easing access to the polls. Citizens are automatically registered and can even update their status online—as late as 8:00 p.m. on Election Day—and everyone votes

IN THE US

JUST **OVER 1/2** OF ELIGIBLE VOTERS VOTE IN PRESIDENTIAL ELECTIONS

UP TO **1/3** OF ELIGIBLE VOTERS AREN'T EVEN REGISTERED

WE HAVE ONE OF THE LOWEST REGISTRATION RATES IN THE WORLD

by mail. Within two years, voter registration rates quadrupled at Oregon's Motor Vehicle Offices. An additional twelve states plus the District of Columbia have approved various ways to register voters automatically. As of 2018, five states, including Kentucky, New York, and Pennsylvania, were considering preregistering sixteen- and seventeen-year-olds, which increases participation in elections.

All but nine other states have proposed legislation or begun ballot initiatives related to such a process. The nine states that have not taken action on automatic registration are Colorado, Delaware, Kansas, Kentucky, Nebraska, New Hampshire, North Dakota, and Wyoming.

Beginning with the midterm elections in 2018, West Virginia offered a novel way for its citizens who live overseas, particularly those in the military, to vote: a blockchain-enabled mobile voting app. This is the technology used for cryptocurrencies. The security of voting by smartphone is being tested.

Other Countries

Canada automatically registers citizens on their eighteenth birthday.

In twenty-four countries, including Belgium, Greece, and Thailand, citizens are *required* to vote! Australians over the age of eighteen, for example, are fined if they don't register and go to the polls. This mandate is controversial. Some Australian politicians argue that it's undemocratic to force people to participate in a democracy. But more than 90 percent of voters there turn out for federal elections.

America's low voter turnout might also be the result of when we vote. In

1845, Congress set Election Day on Tuesday—a work day for many people. Australia, Iceland, New Zealand, and other countries hold elections on Saturday, when fewer people go to work.

Out of a group of fifteen democratic countries, four—Australia, Denmark, New Zealand, and all of the United Kingdom except Northern Ireland—require no ID to vote. Five—Ireland, the Netherlands, Norway, Sweden, and Switzerland—ask for an ID only if there is a reason to doubt the identity of the person who shows up at the polls.

Canada accepts a variety of IDs, none of which needs to include a photo. The remaining countries—Belgium, France, India, Malta, Mexico, and Spain—require photo IDs that are easy to obtain.

Every time an election is held in Spain, an electoral administration helpfully sends everyone who is at least eighteen years old a document telling them where to vote.

The United States
A single nationally run election system

> ### PRINCIPALS CAN DO THE JOB
> State law in Texas requires every high school to hand out voter registration materials to every eligible student at least twice a year, though only about a third of the schools do so.

might limit the crazy-quilt aspect of state election laws. And the Constitution gives Congress the ability to make this fix simply by passing a law. It is unlikely, however, that Congress would pass such legislation because of fears that the political party in power would get the benefit in the short run.

The Story Continues
San Antonio's mayoral election of June 2015 was probably Miller's last opportunity to vote. She died on January 7, 2016, at age 102. Six months later, a federal appeals court ruled that Texas's voter identification law violated the Voting Rights Act because it discriminated against minorities. The law is still in effect, but the court directed the state to help voters obtain the necessary forms of identification.

CHAPTER 9

Who Gets To Represent You?
Restrictions on Running for Congress

What Do You Mean I'm Not Good Enough for You?

Albert Gallatin, a seafaring orphan from Geneva, Switzerland, arrived in Massachusetts in July 1780, at the age of nineteen. He had hoped to farm but discovered that land and seeds cost more than he had reckoned. So he traveled throughout the American colonies, becoming familiar with the terrain and the people. He even joined a militia to help colonists battle the British in Maine, which was then part of Massachusetts.

After the war, he taught French at Harvard College. When he inherited some money, he bought land and built a home in western Pennsylvania.

At the age of twenty-seven, Gallatin entered politics, serving on a committee to evaluate the US Constitution. He was not a fan, believing that it gave too much power to the federal government and not enough to the states. Later he helped revise the Pennsylvania state constitution. Gallatin was then elected to his state's House of Representatives, where he worked on a wide variety of issues, including banking and taxes.

The members of the state legislature recognized Gallatin's expertise in the Constitution, financial matters, and America as a whole. Following the process the Framers had established for selecting senators, the legislature chose him to represent Pennsylvania in the US Senate.

Traveling to Congress in December 1793 was no problem. Both the state and the national capitals were located then in Philadelphia. Taking his seat, however, was another matter.

Gallatin's political opponents challenged his eligibility to serve. He had become an American citizen eight years earlier, in 1785, when he swore allegiance to the Commonwealth of Virginia. But the Constitution required nine years of citizenship before election to the Senate. As a specialist in the Constitution, they pointed out, he should know that.

Gallatin retorted that he'd served in the Revolutionary War in Maine in 1780, thirteen years earlier. Surely his citizenship should count from then.

A majority of his fellow senators disagreed and voted him out. Gallatin lost his seat.

Meanwhile, Back in 1787...

The Framers considered a number of criteria to determine whether someone was eligible to run for Congress. These included the following:

ALBERT GALLATIN TIMELINE

- 1761 – BORN IN SWITZERLAND
- 1780 – ARRIVES IN US
- 1780-1781 SERVES IN AMERICAN MILITIA
- 1785 – BECOMES AN AMERICAN CITIZEN
- 1789 – SERVES IN PENNSYLVANIA STATE LEGISLATURE
- 1790 – ELECTED TO PENNSYLVANIA STATE LEGISLATURE
- 1793 – SELECTED TO REPRESENT PENNSYLVANIA IN THE US SENATE, 8 YEARS AFTER BECOMING A CITIZEN
- 1794 – DECLARED INELIGIBLE TO SERVE IN SENATE, ACCORDING TO HIS OPPONENTS

- residence in the state
- age
- the length of time the person should be a citizen if he was not born in the United States

Some Framers at the Convention argued for another limitation—personal wealth. Charles Pinckney of South Carolina, for instance, proposed that no one could hold office if he didn't own property and cash worth at least $50,000—that's almost $1.4 million today. This requirement would have disqualified more than 99 percent of the population then.

As preposterous as it sounds today, Pinckney's suggestion was taken so seriously that the Framers debated it for three days.

ŝ ŝ

"...some of the greatest rogues
I was ever acquainted with,
were the richest rogues."

—Benjamin Franklin, Pennsylvania

ŝ ŝ

The Framers didn't define citizenship or explain how someone born elsewhere—including several of the Framers themselves—could become a citizen. Nevertheless, they discussed the length of time a candidate for Congress must be a citizen before running. Some Framers pushed for two years for House members and four for senators. George Mason of Virginia, however, warned that allowing recent immigrants

from other countries to hold office would "let foreigners and adventurers make laws for us." They worried especially that British adventurers might come back and take over the country. In any case, James Madison of Virginia argued that senators should be "weaned from the...habits incident to foreign birth and education."

Gouverneur Morris of Pennsylvania wanted to raise the requirement to a minimum of fourteen years of citizenship for both houses. Madison and Benjamin Franklin protested that would prevent too many people from running. In the end, they compromised on seven years for representatives and nine for senators.

On top of that requirement, John Rutledge of South Carolina wanted congressional candidates to have lived in the state they hoped to represent for at least seven years. Otherwise, "an emigrant from New England to South Carolina" could move in and vote however he wanted, even against the

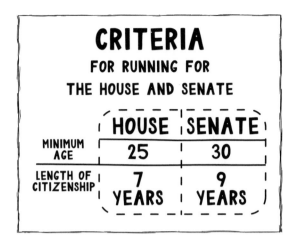

CRITERIA
FOR RUNNING FOR
THE HOUSE AND SENATE

	HOUSE	SENATE
MINIMUM AGE	25	30
LENGTH OF CITIZENSHIP	7 YEARS	9 YEARS

better interests of South Carolinians. Rutledge lost that argument.

❧ ❧

"No person shall be a Representative who shall not have attained to the Age of twenty five Years, and been seven Years a Citizen of the United States, and who shall not, when elected, be an Inhabitant of that State in which he shall be chosen."

—Article I, Section 2

"No Person shall be a Senator who shall not have attained to the Age of thirty Years, and been nine Years a Citizen of the United States, and who shall not, when elected, be an Inhabitant of that State for which he shall be chosen."

—Article I, Section 3

❧ ❧

The Framers didn't explain the age criterion for House members. Madison merely called them "reasonable limitations." During discussions, he justified the higher age for senators than for representatives by saying that senators require "greater extent of information and stability of character."

So What's the Big Problem?

Does our Constitution demand unreasonable residency and age requirements to run for office? By all accounts, Gallatin was a knowledgeable and patriotic American. Should an upstanding citizen be denied the right to serve as a public official? For that matter, should any citizen be prevented from running for office?

SENATOR HIRAM REVELS?

Reverend Hiram Revels nearly missed the honor of becoming our country's first African-American senator.

Following the Civil War, members of the Republican Party set up governments in the defeated Southern states to try to guarantee that formerly enslaved persons would receive the same rights as whites. In 1870, Mississippi's new state senate elected Revels to the US Senate. Democrats, however, didn't want a black man to represent the state in Congress. So they blocked the election, arguing that the Constitution made Revels ineligible for the office.

Even though he had been born in North Carolina forty-three years earlier, his opponents claimed he hadn't been an American citizen for nine years. How could that be?

In an 1857 case called *Dred Scott v. Sandford*, the Supreme Court had ruled that people of African heritage were not citizens. The Fourteenth Amendment overturned that decision, but it was adopted only in 1868, two years before Revels's election. Democrats asserted that he'd been a citizen for only two years.

It was a clever argument, but they lost.

America is often described as a nation of immigrants. But becoming a citizen is a lengthy and complex process. By law, most resident aliens have to live in the country for at least five years before they are eligible for citizenship. As a result, candidates for the House cannot run until they have resided in the country for a minimum of twelve years and candidates for the Senate, a minimum of fourteen. Does it take that long to become familiar with the issues and processes of the federal government?

Minimum age requirements are also hard to justify. If you can vote for your representative and senator at eighteen, why do you have to wait another seven

CAN IMMIGRANTS GET THE JOB DONE?

Albert Gallatin's predicament is not just ancient American history. The same issues cropped up in Georgia in 2018.

Maria Palacios, who was born in Mexico, was barred from running for the State House of Representatives. She had been living in the state since arriving with her parents in 1994, when she was four years old. She became a legal Georgia resident in 2009 and a US citizen in 2017. But, she was kept off the ballot because state law requires that candidates be a citizen there for at least two years, and the secretary of state ruled that a legal resident is not a citizen.

or twelve years before you can run for a seat? And consider the fact that Congress has the power to declare war. Americans can join the military at age eighteen. If you are old enough to serve, shouldn't you be able to participate in the decision about if and where soldiers are deployed?

There Are Other Ways
States

Some states allow young people to run for office, but requirements vary.

Massachusetts, Montana, North Dakota, Ohio, and Vermont have no minimum age requirements to run for the lower house of the state legislature.

Massachusetts requires that candidates for the upper house merely be old enough to vote.

California, Idaho, Kansas, New York, Ohio, Rhode Island, Washington, and Wisconsin allow eighteen-year-olds to run for some offices. In Kansas, that no longer includes governor or lieutenant governor.

States have different requirements—or none at all—for residency. Seven states do not specifically call for a candidate to be a resident to run for their legislatures.

Kansas, Michigan, and New Mexico require simply establishing residency. Rhode Island wants candidates to have lived in the state at least thirty days.

RUN, IF YOU CAN!

Two states—Vermont and Kansas—did not establish a minimum age requirement for running for office. In 2018, young activists took up the challenge for the top spot in both states. Fourteen-year-old Ethan Sonneborn faced off against four opponents, whom he debated on the campaign trail, in his race for the governorship of Vermont. His campaign staff were classmates.

"If I can get one person who wasn't involved in the political process before involved now," he said, "then my campaign will have been a success." On Primary Election Day, he collected more than 8 percent of the statewide vote.

Six teens ran for the same post in Kansas, though only the Democrats allowed their candidate, sixteen-year-old Jack Bergeson, to participate in debates. The state legislature then passed a law setting twenty-five as the minimum age for that office. The first young person to enter the race, Bergeson advised Kansans, "Please go vote! A democracy only works when the citizens are engaged in the process."

Other mandates for running for the state Senate range from requiring one year of residence in Idaho, to seven years in New Hampshire.

Other Countries

In some countries, any citizen can run for election, regardless of the source or length of their citizenship. Examples include Belgium and Ireland.

Also in some countries, if candidates are old enough to vote, they can run for office, though usually not for head of state. This is the case, for instance, in Australia, Britain, Germany, Iceland, and New Zealand. The same is true for eighteen-year-olds in France who want to run for the lower house of Parliament, but *citoyens* there must be at least twenty-four to run for the Senate.

Other countries allow their citizens to run for office a few years after they reach minimum voting age. In Austria, the period is two years, and in Belgium, Ireland, and Luxembourg, three years.

The United States

In order to eliminate candidacy requirements for age, length of residency, and citizenship, we would have to amend the Constitution. Because there is no widespread call to do so, it will probably be up to young people, newcomers, and recent citizens to push for this change.

The Story Continues

After being ousted from the Senate, Gallatin ran for a seat in the House of Representatives, which required only seven years of citizenship. He was elected in November 1794.

He became an important leader of the Democratic-Republican Party, headed by Thomas Jefferson. Upon becoming president in 1801, Jefferson named Gallatin Secretary of the Treasury.

When Madison became president eight years later, he asked Gallatin to stay on, and the man who had worked so hard for his adopted country continued to serve until 1814. He holds the record for having served the longest term as Secretary of the Treasury, one of the most important departments within the executive branch.

CHAPTER 10

Who Gets a Shot at the Oval Office?
Restrictions on Running for President

"The Honorable Thing to Do"

The son of an active-duty, four-star Navy admiral, John Sidney McCain III was born in 1936 in the Panama Canal Zone, then a US territory. He grew up on naval bases in America and abroad. After graduating from high school in Virginia, he followed a family tradition of military service by enrolling in the Naval Academy; the young plebe's grandfather had also been a four-star admiral.

In 1966, McCain volunteered to fly bombing missions in the war the United States was fighting against Communists in North Vietnam. The following year, his plane was shot down over Hanoi, the capital, and, with a broken leg and two broken arms, he was taken prisoner.

He spent five and a half brutal years in captivity—three and a half of them in solitary confinement—and was regularly beaten and tortured. Although his captors repeatedly offered to let him go, he refused. The military Code of Conduct directed that another pilot, imprisoned earlier, should be released first.

"I just didn't think it was the honorable thing to do," McCain later explained. Two months after a cease-fire ended hostilities between America and North Vietnam in 1973, McCain finally came home.

Despite earning multiple medals, including the Silver Star, the Bronze Star, and the Legion of Merit, he realized his injuries prevented him from advancing in his career, and he left the military. He decided to serve his country in another way. McCain entered politics as a Republican in Arizona, where he had moved, and, in 1982, won a seat in the House of Representatives. After serving two terms in the House, he was elected to the Senate. Then, in 2008, McCain ran for the presidency. It wasn't clear, however, that he would be allowed to serve if he won.

At the time he was born, Congress had not yet passed a statute declaring that children of American citizens born in the Canal Zone would automatically be US citizens. That didn't happen until six months later.

The Constitution requires that our executive be a "natural born Citizen" and "been fourteen years a resident of the United States." Unfortunately, no one knows exactly what those terms mean or whether they necessarily fit someone born in a US territory.

During his campaign, McCain asked prominent constitutional lawyers to analyze the situation. They concluded that he met the definition of a "natural born Citizen" but their opinion didn't amount to a final, binding decision. If McCain won, opponents might have contested his eligibility to become president.

Meanwhile, Back in 1787...

The Framers didn't just make the obstacles for the presidency higher than those for Congress. They also made them incomprehensible. John Jay, who had served as president of the Continental Congress but did not attend the Constitutional Convention, explained that candidates should be old enough for voters to be able to judge their true character. Younger men might deceive voters with "brilliant appearances of genius and patriotism, which...sometimes mislead as well as dazzle."

As for the fourteen-year residency, Jay wrote that presidents "should continue in place a sufficient time to become perfectly acquainted with our national concerns."

Jay is also probably the source of

a stipulation about the citizenship of presidential hopefuls. In 1787, he wrote to George Washington, "the commander in chief of the American army shall not be given to, nor devolve on, any but a natural born citizen." Shortly thereafter, the phrase "natural born citizen," whatever it means, found its way into our Constitution. Washington and the other Framers were probably worried about an outsider taking charge, but they cared more about foreign-born interlopers than clarity.

☙ ❧

"No person except a natural born Citizen, or a Citizen of the United States, at the time of the Adoption of this Constitution, shall be eligible to the Office of President; neither shall any Person be eligible to that Office who shall not have attained to the Age of thirty five Years, and been fourteen Years a Resident within the United States."

—Article II, Section 1

☙ ❧

So What's the Big Problem?

Americans proudly say that anyone can grow up to be president. But that's not necessarily the case. The United States puts more limitations on running for the presidency than any other democratic country. As a result, we might miss some good candidates.

Jennifer Granholm came to the United States from Canada with her parents in 1963 when she was four years old. She became a citizen when she was twenty-one. In 2003, she was inaugurated as the first female governor of

1/3 OF AMERICAN CITIZENS ARE INELIGIBLE TO BECOME PRESIDENT BECAUSE OF THE RESTRICTIONS IN OUR CONSTITUTION AND BECAUSE OF THE LARGE NUMBER OF IMMIGRANTS

Michigan. Unless the Constitution is amended, Granholm will never be eligible to serve as president of the United States.

Many people might have supported California Governor Arnold Schwarzenegger for president in 2008, but he was ineligible because he was born in Austria and became an American citizen as a teenager.

Naturalized citizens (those who were born abroad but became legal citizens of the United States) have served in Congress, as members of the Supreme Court and presidential cabinets, and as head of the Joint Chiefs of Staff of the United States military. The only offices barred to those who are not US citizens at birth are the presidency—and the vice presidency, in case that person ultimately has to serve as president.

Furthermore, what's magical about the age of thirty-five? Just as with candidates for Congress, couldn't many younger people be qualified to run for the office?

PRIME MINISTER WHIPPERSNAPPER

At the time the Americans were drafting the constitutional clauses covering eligibility for office, the British prime minister was William Pitt the Younger. He was called that not only because his father, who had the same name, had also been prime minister, but also because he himself was only twenty-four when he became prime minister.

There Are Other Ways
States

While the president is the chief executive of the country, the chief in every state is the governor. And states vary widely in their residency, citizenship, and age requirements for this office.

Many states require state residency for a minimum period:

- California, Louisiana, Maine, and Texas: five years
- Alabama and Florida: seven years
- Missouri: ten years

Some states also have citizenship requirements:

• California requires candidates for governor to have been American citizens for at least five years and Georgia for fifteen years.

• New Jersey demands twenty years of US citizenship.

States have varied age requirements:

• Thirty-five states, including Arkansas, Florida, and Pennsylvania, set the minimum age at thirty.

• Five allow anyone who is old enough to vote to run for the executive slot.

Other Countries

In most countries, any citizen can run for head of state. However, Bhutan, Brazil, Mexico, Peru, the Philippines, Tunisia, Zambia, and several Latin American countries do require presidents to be natural-born citizens.

Most countries also set a minimum age, ranging from eighteen in Australia, France, and Britain to fifty in Italy.

France also mandates that a presidential candidate have a bank account!

Thirty countries stipulate that their leaders must belong to a particular religion. Andorra and Lebanon require their leaders to be Christian. Bhutan and Thailand only allow Buddhist leaders. Iran, Jordan, Morocco, Saudi Arabia, and Syria require leaders to be Muslim.

The United States

The Constitution would need to be amended to change age and citizenship requirements.

The Story Continues

McCain failed to win the presidential election, losing to Barack Obama, so his status as a natural-born citizen was not tested in court. In 2008, the Senate unanimously passed a resolution declaring McCain a natural-born citizen.

The problem arose again in 2016, when Texas Senator Ted Cruz ran for the Republican presidential nomination. Cruz was born in Canada to an

American mother and Cuban father. According to federal law, he was a citizen at birth because his mother had met the requirements for passing on citizenship to her children. She was born in the United States and lived there for at least four years after turning age fourteen. That fact did not stop some people from asserting that he was not "natural born" under the Constitution because he needed help from that law to run. Lawyers were split on the issue, though most argued that he met the standard.

Since Cruz failed in his quest for the nomination, we still don't know for sure whether a citizen born outside the continental United States or Hawaii would be eligible to serve as president.

CHAPTER 11

Time's Up!
Presidential Term Limits

"No Ordinary Time"

In the spring and summer of 1940, the news from Europe was becoming more frightening practically by the minute. In the previous twelve months, Germany had annexed Austria and parts of Czechoslovakia and then invaded Poland. Immediately after that, Britain and France declared war on Germany. Then, in April and May of 1940, the Nazis invaded Denmark, Belgium, Luxembourg, the Netherlands, and Norway. On June 14, Paris, the glorious capital of France, fell to the marauding enemy.

Most Americans were struggling under the decadelong economic Great Depression and wanted nothing to do with the war in Europe. They were still disillusioned by President Woodrow Wilson's decision to enter World War I in 1917, even though he had promised not to.

These were hard times. Many voters were glad that President Franklin Delano Roosevelt was nearing the end of his second term as president. They assumed he wouldn't run again. After all, George Washington, not wanting to look like a monarch, had declined to run a third time after eight years in office. Weren't presidents limited to two terms?

No, they weren't. A third presidential term wasn't illegal or unconstitutional.

Roosevelt begged to disagree with those who said he should gracefully depart at the end of his second term.

He believed no one else knew as much about the troubling and complex issues at home and abroad as he did. The country could be at grave risk; a new president would have to learn the ropes on the job.

৶ ৶

"If Great Britain goes down, all of us in all of the Americas would be living at the point of a gun."

—President Franklin Delano Roosevelt

৶ ৶

Roosevelt didn't admit publicly that he wanted to stay in the White House. Multiple candidates jockeyed to win the nomination. On July 15, the first day of the Democratic Convention in the Chicago Stadium, FDR had Senator Alben Barkley read a statement saying that Roosevelt did not want to continue as president and the Convention should feel free to choose another candidate. The delegates were stunned into silence.

At that moment, a chant boomed over the loudspeakers. "America

> ## "AN UNWRITTEN CONSTITUTION"
> We tend to assume that, because something has been done a certain way for a long time, it has to be that way. For instance, we're used to seeing nine justices on the Supreme Court, even though the Constitution does not require that number. Nor does it stipulate that the president has to live in the White House.

wants Roosevelt! Humanity wants Roosevelt!" The voice belonged to Thomas D. Garry, Chicago's Superintendent of Sanitation, who, by prior arrangement with Chicago Mayor Edward J. Kelly and probably FDR, shouted into a microphone in the basement. Garry became known as the "voice from the sewers."

The conventioneers picked up the refrain. Still, many were uneasy about the notion of a third-term president. It just didn't seem right, given the long-standing precedent.

The next day, First Lady Eleanor Roosevelt flew to Chicago and spoke to

WENDELL WILLKIE

THE REPUBLICAN PARTY'S NOMINEE WHO RAN AGAINST FDR DISTRIBUTED CAMPAIGN BUTTONS READING

NO THIRD TERM

STRIKE 3 YOU'RE OUT

ROOSEVELT FOR EX PRESIDENT

the crowd. "This is no ordinary time," she stated, referring to the extraordinary troubles at home and abroad. Immediately after Mrs. Roosevelt's speech, her husband won the nomination with support from 86 percent of the delegates.

Although more than twenty-two million Americans voted against him, Roosevelt won the November election—and a third term—with nearly 55 percent of the vote.

Meanwhile, Back in ~~1787~~ 1951...

The length of the president's term and the number of times, if any, that

he could be reelected were issues as important to the Framers as his powers. Allow him to be president for life and he might as well be king. Too short a presidency and he wouldn't accomplish anything. They brainstormed and batted around practically every possible option regarding the number and length of terms, as well as approaches for how the president would be chosen.

Hugh Williamson of North Carolina proposed three presidents, each from a different part of the country, all serving together for twelve years. The president from the slave states could square off against the one from the free states, with the mid-Atlantic president trying to keep the peace.

Elbridge Gerry of Massachusetts feared the president would cave in to Congress if that body appointed him. So he argued for one president serving a single term with no possibility of reelection. Most of all, the Framers wanted to block any chance of anointing a monarch. They weren't optimistic they'd succeed, though.

In a six-hour lecture, Alexander Hamilton of New York even called for "an elected monarch" chosen by electors for the rest of his life. The Framers met his plan with silence but very nearly adopted Williamson's.

If the president wouldn't serve for life, then how long? Six years? Seven? How about eleven, fifteen, or twenty years? All of these were discussed, though James Wilson of Pennsylvania pronounced the longer proposed terms ridiculous.

Or, as James McClurg of Virginia, a doctor with absolutely no political experience, suggested, maybe the president should be appointed by Congress and serve as long as he showed "good behavior." Gouverneur Morris of Pennsylvania enthusiastically endorsed this idea, exclaiming, "This is the way to get a good government." Their reasoning was that the chief executive wouldn't be able to push his weight around if he had to keep Congress happy in order to hold onto his job. This plan, too, was nearly adopted until the Framers

concluded that a president with no term limit could become too powerful.

୨ ଏ

"…it was pretty certain… that we should at some time or other have a King."
—Hugh Williamson, North Carolina

୨ ଏ

Delegates voted, sometimes multiple times, on all of these suggestions. After three months of debating, negotiating, voting, switching votes, delaying, reopening, and redebating the issue, the Framers finally settled, just a week before they adjourned, on the system that we now take for granted—a presidential term of four years.

୨ ଏ

"The executive Power shall be vested in a President of the United States of America. He shall hold his Office during the term of four years…"
—Article II, Section 1

୨ ଏ

GET HIM OUTTA THERE!

Four or eight years might be the appropriate length of time for most presidents to serve. But what if the electorate realizes after a year or two that the person in the Oval Office poses a danger to the country? Are we stuck with them?

The Constitution provides a way for Congress to impeach and hold a trial if the president is suspected of committing a "high crime or misdemeanor." Otherwise, if the commander in chief is merely reckless or incompetent or terrifying, we have no way out.

Parliamentary systems, on the other hand, allow the legislature to declare a vote of no confidence in the head of government. In this case, the leader is out of the job no matter how long they have been in office.

Note that the Framers did not deal with whether or not the president could be reelected, let alone for the number of terms. That can got kicked down the road until 1947, when Congress proposed the Twenty-second Amendment, which was adopted in 1951 in response to Roosevelt's multiple elections.

"No person shall be elected to the office of the President more than twice, and no person who has held the office of President, or acted as President, for more than two years of a term to which some other person was elected President shall be elected to the office of the President more than once."

—Twenty-second Amendment, Section 1

So What's the Big Problem?

The 1787 Constitution was silent on presidential term limits. The Framers' decision not to make a decision meant that neither presidents nor the public were sure of the ground rules. Were there circumstances under which the executive could stay in office forever? Until Roosevelt, the answer seemed to be no. But no one knew for sure.

When Roosevelt shattered tradition by running for a third and then a fourth term, it appeared that the Framers' initial fears—and Williamson's prediction—might have been justified. Perhaps America would be ruled by a monarch after all.

The Twenty-second Amendment both resolved the uncertainty and eliminated the possibility of a president for life by limiting the number of presidential terms to two. But this amendment contains a downside. A presidency of more than ten years is impossible—and even a ten-year term can happen only when a vice president takes over in the second half of a president's four-year term. As Eleanor Roosevelt suggested, this constitutional prohibition could turn into a genuine fault line in times of war, severe depression, or other catastrophe. At these times, we might well need a knowledgeable and experienced leader—but we might not be able to keep them.

OTHER PRESIDENTS ALSO CONSIDERED RUNNING FOR MORE THAN 2 TERMS

ULYSSES S. GRANT WANTED TO RUN FOR A 3RD TERM IN 1880 BUT HIS PARTY REFUSED TO NOMINATE HIM

THEODORE ROOSEVELT RAN UNSUCCESSFULLY FOR A 3RD TERM IN 1912 AS A THIRD-PARTY CANDIDATE AFTER BEING OUT OF OFFICE FOR 4 YEARS

FDR'S DISTANT COUSIN

There Are Other Ways
States

Only fourteen states allow their chief executives—governors—to serve as long as the voters want them to stay in office. The other thirty-six states impose term limits of various sorts on their governors.

Eight of these, including Delaware,

JUSTICE FOR LIFE

The president loses his job after two terms. Congresspeople can be thrown out at any election. Judges are a different matter.

The Constitution states, "The Judges, both of the supreme and inferior Courts, shall hold their Offices during good Behaviour." The term "good Behaviour" is not defined but is taken to mean that a judge cannot be impeached because they hands down an unpopular decision. This supports the idea of judicial independence, meaning that judges can enforce the Constitution however they see fit.

This provision in the Constitution is also generally interpreted to mean that, once they're appointed, judges can stay on the bench as long as they want. Supreme Court Justice John Paul Stevens, for example, retired at age ninety after serving for thirty-four years.

All but one state and most other countries force judges to retire at a certain age or after a number of years on the job.

Missouri, and Oklahoma, bar governors from serving more than twice.

Almost two dozen others, including Alaska, Hawaii, New Mexico, and West Virginia, allow governors to serve more than two times but only after they've been out of office for at least one term.

Indiana, Montana, Wyoming, and a few other states impose a limit of eight years out of every twelve or sixteen.

Other Countries

In countries with parliamentary systems, such as Germany, India, Israel, Japan, and the United Kingdom, the legislature appoints or elects the head of government. The prime minister keeps the job until defeated in an election, until resignation, or until the parliament votes that it has "no confidence" in them.

Other democracies without presidential term limits include Germany, Iceland, and India.

Many others, such as Austria and France, do impose limits, usually two terms.

The United States

Ideally, Congress would have the ability to suspend the two-term rule—or the four-year-term rule—under exceptional circumstances, perhaps by a two-thirds vote. Such circumstances might include wars or other national catastrophes. This procedure would require amending the Constitution.

The Story Continues

Four years later, with America at war, Roosevelt won yet again. He was the first—and last— president to be elected to office four times. His Republican opponents, who took over the House and the Senate in 1947, wanted to be sure a Democrat would never again stay in office so long and proposed the Twenty-second Amendment.

PART IV

"Hurrah! I'm 18. Finally I Can Vote For the President." "Not So Fast."

Americans don't vote directly for our president. Instead, we vote for individuals who represent our voting preferences—we hope—in an organization informally called the Electoral College.

We vote for the members of this group at the state level (not the national level), but the number of members in each state does not exactly reflect the size of its population. Some states count more than others—literally.

States also handle the results of their Electoral College votes differently. Presidential elections can indicate which candidate voters across the country prefer. But the Electoral College sometimes doesn't let the more popular candidate become president.

There are reasons the Framers did not choose to pick our commander through direct election, which is the way we elect other leaders. Even when the Constitution was drafted, this process was controversial. But you're reading this book in the twenty-first century, and reasons that might have seemed logical in 1787 do not necessarily make sense more than two centuries later.

The single chapter in Part IV explains a whopper of a fault line in our Constitution.

CHAPTER 12

The College with No Courses or Credits
The Electoral College

"We Got a Problem Here"

On the evening of Tuesday, November 7, 2000, Vice President Al Gore Jr. and his family gathered in Nashville, Tennessee, to watch election returns on television. Gore, a former senator from that state, topped the Democratic ticket for the presidency.

He knew—in fact the whole country knew—that the race would be close. The Republican nominee was George W. Bush, the popular governor of Texas and son of former president George H. W. Bush. In the final weeks of the campaign, some polls favored Gore; others, Bush. The outcome could still tip either way.

As polling places closed from the East Coast toward the West Coast, television newscasters aired interviews with voters to get an idea of the results before all the votes were counted. These exit polls indicated that 49 percent of voters had supported Gore and only 48 percent had picked Bush. Democrats had good reason to believe they'd keep the White House.

At 7:49 p.m. Eastern Standard Time, the major television networks called Florida for Gore—that is, they predicted that he would get more votes than anyone else.

Two hours later, networks also called New Mexico for Gore. That put him over the top!

Even though the polls hadn't closed

everywhere, it appeared Gore would be elected the next president of the United States. The Gores, his running mate Joe Lieberman, and their staffs whooped in victory. They were so gleeful, one journalist said, "There was pandemonium."

Seven minutes after that, however, Nick Baldick, a campaign worker responsible for following the results in Florida, urged caution. "We got a problem here," he said. "This is going to be really close."

He was examining the vote totals in certain Florida precincts. Because he knew which neighborhoods had more Democrats and which had more Republicans, he believed he could predict the outcomes. It was on the basis of such predictions that the networks had projected Gore would win the state.

As results came in, though, some precincts that everyone had expected to support Gore ended up favoring Bush.

Since the Democrats could no longer count on what they had presumed were reliably Democratic precincts, Baldick alerted Gore and the other staffers that the race was too close to call before every single vote was counted. In fact, they might lose after all. That warning ended what a spokesman called "our seven-minute presidency."

Bush was beating Gore in Florida by about fifty thousand votes. But across the country, it looked as if Gore was beating Bush by about half a million votes.

Why was Baldick worried? Gore should win the election, no matter which way Florida tilted, right?

Meanwhile, Back in 1787 (and 1804)...

Initially the delegates to the Constitutional Convention didn't know what to call the leader of their fledgling country—Executive Magistracy was one unwieldy option—or even how many leaders they'd need. One? Three?

The only experience they had was rule by a hereditary monarch, a system they loathed. There was a myriad number of alternatives to a king, yet the specifics were hard to imagine.

Despite their fears of establishing another monarchy, it took only a few weeks for the majority of the Framers to determine that the country should be led by a single individual. Over the next three months, they voted at least sixty times on different ways to choose that person. Methods varied in part depending on which powers delegates felt the leader should have.

Roger Sherman of Connecticut argued that the legislative branch should carry more weight than the executive. Therefore, Congress should choose the leader.

Elbridge Gerry of Massachusetts, Gunning Bedford of Delaware, and others worried that under Sherman's scheme, the national government would overshadow the states. They contended that state legislatures should do the picking.

James Wilson of Pennsylvania proposed direct election—a system in which the president would be selected by eligible voters.

But no one agreed with Wilson.

"I have ever observed that a choice by the people themselves is not generally distinguished for its wisdom."

—Thomas Jefferson

There was a somewhat understandable reason for the opponents' view. America was a very different place in 1787.

The roughly three and a half million Americans were dispersed across a vast terrain—as much territory as Britain, France, Germany, Ireland, and Italy combined. Fewer than one hundred newspapers were published in the country, and none was widely distributed. Papers contained only four pages, half of them devoted to advertisements and the other half to local news. Men in South Carolina, say, would probably know nothing about a candidate from Pennsylvania.

In September, after months of wrangling, the Framers were all set to adopt Sherman's idea for Congress to elect the president. At that moment, John Dickinson of Delaware, who had been absent for much of the previous five weeks, reappeared, heard the proposal, and expressed his alarm. Such a plan would give too much power to Congress. In any case, he warned, people would never ratify the Constitution unless they were somehow involved in choosing the president. Yet again, the Convention was in disarray.

James Madison of Virginia took pen and paper and wrote out a complicated alternative, calling for a system of presidential electors. Each state's legislature would decide how to select a group of trustworthy individuals. These electors would then vote for the person they considered most worthy of serving as president. To account for the differences in sizes of the states, each would be allowed as many electors as the sum of its representatives plus its two senators.

By now, the Framers, who had rejected every other notion, were ready to accept this one. They signed on to the plan ten days before adjourning and spent the next several days cranking out the details.

৵ ৶

"The executive Power shall be vested in a President of the United States of America. He shall hold his Office during the Term of four Years, and, together with the Vice President, chosen for the same Term, be elected, as follows:

Each State shall appoint, in such Manner as the Legislature thereof may direct, a Number of Electors, equal to the whole Number of Senators and Representatives to which the State may be entitled in the Congress: but no Senator or Representative, or Person holding an Office of Trust or Profit under the United States, shall be appointed an Elector."

—Article II, Section 1

৵ ৶

This arrangement, which later came to be called the Electoral College, was popular with small states. Even the tiniest of them got three electoral votes.

Slaveholding states, especially those in the South with large numbers of enslaved people, liked the Electoral College as well. Under the terms of the Three-Fifths Compromise, slave states got to count not only white citizens as part of their population, but also three-fifths of their enslaved persons. As a result, they received both more representatives in Congress and more electors. This deal expanded their influence in choosing the president.

Of course, enslaved people, like women and children, couldn't vote. Southern gentlemen claimed they would keep the best interests of women and children in mind when they voted, but none cared about their slaves' desires or opinions. The Electoral College, however, made the actual numbers of voters in a given state irrelevant.

In short order, the Framers decided on the following rules.

• Electors in every state would meet on a day set by Congress and vote for their two favorite candidates.

• The electors' votes from all the states would be compiled. A majority of the electors had to agree on a single candidate. The winner would become president; the runner-up would become vice president.

• In case no single candidate received a majority of the electoral votes, the House of Representatives would choose the president from the top five vote-getters, with each state casting one vote. If the representatives from a state were evenly split in their choice, the state would be listed as abstaining. The Senate would choose the vice president.

The Framers thought they had finally figured out how to pick a leader. And the Electoral College worked fine as long as George Washington, who was elected twice unanimously, was president. But he refused to serve a third term, and the Framers' system hit a snag in the very next election.

Party Politics

By 1796, political parties had begun to form, and the electors' top two favorite candidates belonged to different ones.

President John Adams was a Federalist. But the runner-up, Vice President Thomas Jefferson, was a Democratic-Republican.

American politics were as split then as they are now. Today, this would be like having a conservative member of the Republican Party as president and a liberal Democrat as vice president. The vice president, who can break tie votes as president of the Senate, might vote against the president's Supreme Court nominees and otherwise undermine his policies.

In fact, that's exactly what happened. A year after their inauguration, Jefferson turned on Adams.

In 1798, Adams signed the Alien and Sedition Acts into law. Supported by the Federalist Party, the Sedition Acts made it a crime to criticize the president—but said nothing about criticizing the vice president!

Jefferson was appalled by the legislation. He secretly wrote documents that argued that state legislatures could declare federal laws unconstitutional. In 1798, the Kentucky legislature adopted these so-called Kentucky Resolutions. These actions triggered a debate about who gets to decide whether a law is constitutional—an issue that has never been completely resolved. However, the Adams administration disagreed with Jefferson's claim and successfully prosecuted some Democratic newspaper editors for sedition. When Jefferson became president in 1801, he pardoned them.

Tie Vote

Jefferson's own election in 1800, revealed another flaw in the Electoral College—one so grave it nearly resulted in civil war. There were four candidates: Jefferson and Aaron Burr on the Democratic-Republican side against Adams and Charles Pinckney on the Federalist side. Whichever man won the most votes in the Electoral College, as long as he got a majority, would become president.

When the votes were tallied, it turned out that both Jefferson and

Burr got a majority, but they were tied. Since the Electoral College hadn't agreed on a single candidate, there was no winner. Under these circumstances, the Constitution directed the House of Representatives to pick the president.

Many members of the House were Federalists who had just been voted out of office—but their terms didn't expire until Inauguration Day, March 4, 1801. Because of the process described in the Constitution, departing representatives would pick the incoming president.

The House voted thirty-six times over six days before coming to an agreement. That happened only when James A. Bayard, along with other Federalists, abstained, tilting the election to Jefferson. Bayard might have done this because the governors of Virginia and Pennsylvania, both Democratic-Republicans, threatened to march their militias on the national Capitol if Jefferson wasn't chosen.

After that near calamity, Congress proposed and the state legislatures ratified the Twelfth Amendment in time for the election of 1804. This amendment changed the system: electors would now cast two separate votes, one for president and the other for vice president. If the Electoral College did not produce a majority winner, then the House would determine the presidency by choosing among the top three vote-getters, not among the top five, as before.

Winners Become Losers

Twenty years later, the problems with this supposed solution became clear. In 1824, Andrew Jackson became the first candidate to win both the most popular—that is, the people's votes—and the most electoral votes but still lose the presidency. Remember: the people's votes don't matter; only the electoral votes count, and the Electoral College requires a majority, not just the most votes.

There were four contenders: Jackson, John Quincy Adams, William H. Crawford, and Henry Clay. Because none of them got a majority, the decision was thrown into the House of Representatives. Clay, who wasn't eligible because he came in fourth, lobbied the representatives to pick Adams, which they did. Adams then named Clay his Secretary of State. Furious, Jackson called the decision "a corrupt bargain."

The next winner to lose was the Democratic candidate Samuel J. Tilden in 1876. By midnight on Election Day, he was ahead of his opponent, Rutherford B. Hayes, a Republican, by 250,000 votes and had amassed 184 of the 185 necessary Electoral College votes. But, the counts in three southern states were in dispute, and Hayes refused to concede. Finally, in March 1877, the parties reached a compromise. Reconstruction policies in the South ended; in exchange, the presidency was handed to Hayes, who became known as "His Fraudulency."

So What's the Big Problem?

The national popularity of a presidential candidate in the November election has little—sometimes nothing—to do with who becomes president the following January.

Let's Do the Math

Running for president is a math problem in which the greatest variable is the Electoral College.

To become president, a candidate needs to win the popular vote in the right combination of states—those whose Electoral College votes will add up to 270, a majority. Calculating ways to achieve this number can cause campaign shenanigans.

Thanks to the Electoral College, a presidential candidate could win the vote of every person in thirty-nine states and the District of Columbia and still lose the general election. That's because the Electoral College votes from a combination of eleven specific states add up to the necessary total of 270.

Little States, Big Say

Nationwide, twenty-six states have a higher percentage of electoral votes

538
MEMBERS OF THE
ELECTORAL COLLEGE
=
435
1 FOR EACH MEMBER
OF THE HOUSE
+
100
1 FOR EACH MEMBER
OF THE SENATE
+
3
FOR DC, WHICH WERE GRANTED IN
THE 23RD AMENDMENT IN 1961

In 2016, California was home to thirty-nine million people—about two million more than the twenty-one smallest states plus DC combined. Yet, in that presidential election, California got fifty-five electoral votes while those twenty-one states plus DC got a total of ninety-five. That's because of the boost they received from their senators.

Wyoming and North and South Dakota got a total of nine electoral votes while New Mexico, whose population was about the same as those three states put together, got only five.

Winner Take All

In all but two states—Maine and Nebraska—the candidate who wins the most popular votes amasses all of that than is warranted by their percentage of the population.

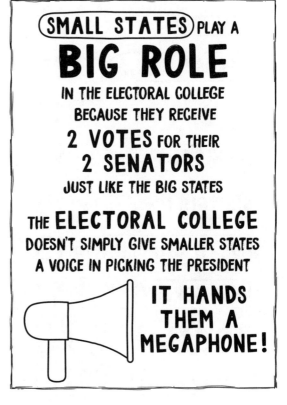

SMALL STATES PLAY A
BIG ROLE
IN THE ELECTORAL COLLEGE
BECAUSE THEY RECEIVE
2 VOTES FOR THEIR
2 SENATORS
JUST LIKE THE BIG STATES

THE **ELECTORAL COLLEGE**
DOESN'T SIMPLY GIVE SMALLER STATES
A VOICE IN PICKING THE PRESIDENT
**IT HANDS
THEM A
MEGAPHONE!**

YOU COULD WIN JUST THESE 11 STATES BY EXTREMELY NARROW MARGINS AND BECOME PRESIDENT, EVEN IF YOU FAILED TO GET A SINGLE VOTE IN ANY OTHER STATE

CALIFORNIA - - - - 55

TEXAS - - - - - - 38

NEW YORK - - - - 29

FLORIDA - - - - - 29

ILLINOIS - - - - - 20

PENNSYLVANIA - - 20

OHIO - - - - - - - 18

MICHIGAN - - - - 16

GEORGIA - - - - - 16

NORTH CAROLINA - 15

NEW JERSEY - - - 14

TOTAL - - - 270 ELECTORAL VOTES

state's Electoral College votes. The winner doesn't even need to get a majority of the votes in the state—only to come in ahead of everyone else.

This problem goes way back and carries serious implications. Nearly ten million people voted in the election of 1884. If only 575 residents of New York had switched their votes, America would have been led by President James G. Blaine instead of Grover Cleveland. Had the Electoral College votes in the 2016 election been allocated proportionately, Hillary Rodham Clinton would have received two more votes than Donald J. Trump—but not a majority because of third-party candidates. As a result, the House of Representatives would have chosen the president.

Battleground States

Individual voters in presidential elections don't matter much—states do. But not very many states.

Presidential candidates have to calculate where to spend their time and

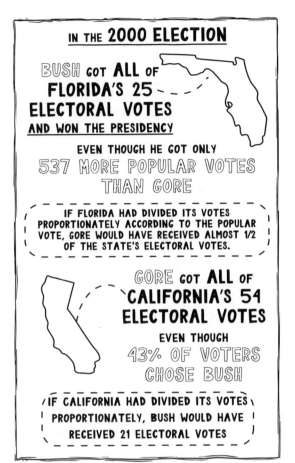

IN THE **2000 ELECTION**

BUSH GOT **ALL OF FLORIDA'S 25 ELECTORAL VOTES** AND WON THE PRESIDENCY

EVEN THOUGH HE GOT ONLY 537 MORE POPULAR VOTES THAN GORE

IF FLORIDA HAD DIVIDED ITS VOTES PROPORTIONATELY ACCORDING TO THE POPULAR VOTE, GORE WOULD HAVE RECEIVED ALMOST 1/2 OF THE STATE'S ELECTORAL VOTES.

GORE GOT **ALL OF CALIFORNIA'S 54 ELECTORAL VOTES**

EVEN THOUGH 43% OF VOTERS CHOSE BUSH

IF CALIFORNIA HAD DIVIDED ITS VOTES PROPORTIONATELY, BUSH WOULD HAVE RECEIVED 21 ELECTORAL VOTES

focus on the states that will tip their Electoral College counts into the winning column. These unpredictable states where the contest rages are called battleground or swing states. Voters in most of the rest of the country never have a chance to hear a candidate speak at a local campaign stop.

The Electoral College not only picks the president, it also influences the campaigns. Only one of the country's ten largest cities—Philadelphia, Pennsylvania—is located in a battleground state, so urban issues are addressed far less often than matters that concern battleground residents.

Why Bother?

Because their issues aren't discussed and their votes barely count, many eligible voters in non-battleground states may feel discouraged from going to the polls. Why take the time to vote if the Electoral College votes are likely to go to a different candidate? And after all, the candidates didn't go out of their way to ask them for their votes.

money and which issues to emphasize during their campaign. It makes sense for them to pay closer attention to states in which the results are a toss-up—especially those with lots of Electoral College votes—rather than states they're confident they'll win whether or not they campaign there.

Instead of running national campaigns directed to all voters, candidates

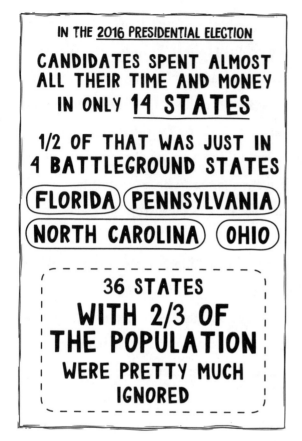

IN THE 2016 PRESIDENTIAL ELECTION

CANDIDATES SPENT ALMOST ALL THEIR TIME AND MONEY IN ONLY **14 STATES**

1/2 OF THAT WAS JUST IN 4 BATTLEGROUND STATES

FLORIDA   PENNSYLVANIA
NORTH CAROLINA   OHIO

36 STATES **WITH 2/3 OF THE POPULATION** WERE PRETTY MUCH IGNORED

IN 2016

OVER **65%** OF ELIGIBLE VOTERS IN SWING STATES VOTED.

ONLY **56%** OF ELIGIBLE VOTERS IN OTHER STATES VOTED.

OVERALL, ONLY **58%** OF REGISTERED VOTERS VOTED.

The popular vote reflects the preferences only of those who show up to vote. It does not necessarily reflect the views of the electorate as a whole.

Faithless Electors

The Constitution says nothing about requiring members of the Electoral College to vote the way the citizens have told them to. However, laws in twenty-nine states and the District of Columbia control how electors can vote. Some lawyers believe these are unconstitutional because the Framers put their faith in the independent judgment of electors. In the other twenty-one states, electors can vote for whomever they like.

Those who go rogue have come to be called faithless electors. After the

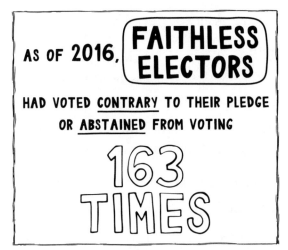

AS OF 2016, **FAITHLESS ELECTORS** HAD VOTED <u>CONTRARY</u> TO THEIR PLEDGE OR <u>ABSTAINED</u> FROM VOTING

163 TIMES

2016 election, some opponents of Donald J. Trump, who viewed him as unfit to be president, encouraged Republican electors to use their independent judgment by voting for another Republican rather than Trump. Two Texas electors did so.

So far, no faithless elector has influenced the outcome of a presidential election. Nevertheless, it is possible that they could overturn an election, and no one could stop them.

What If No One Wins?

If no one wins a majority of the electoral votes, the plan that the Framers devised remains on the books. The House of Representatives picks the president, and the Senate chooses the vice president.

This sounds straightforward, but the constitutional process could drive us straight into a ditch. The House could choose a Republican president while the Senate chooses a Democratic vice president. The country would be no better off than it was in 1796, when President John Adams was a Federalist while Vice President Thomas Jefferson was a Democratic-Republican.

EVEN THE CANDIDATES HATE THE ELECTORAL COLLEGE

Long before they ran against each other for the presidency, both Hillary Rodham Clinton and Donald J. Trump had criticized the Electoral College.

"It's time to do away with the Electoral College and move to the popular election of our president."
—Hillary Rodham Clinton, 2000

"The Electoral College is a disaster for a democracy."
—Donald J. Trump, 2012

Or maybe the Senate would end up choosing the president after all. Here's how that could happen.

When the House chooses the president, each state is entitled to cast one vote. That means that a majority of each state's representatives in the House must agree on whom to vote for. If a state's legislators are evenly divided between two candidates, then all of the representatives from that state have to abstain. The state loses its right to vote for president. This can make it harder for the leading candidate to get the necessary majority of states.

In order to reach a majority, a candidate must receive the votes of twenty-six states. If enough states abstain so that the House cannot choose a president—and the Senate has chosen a vice president from only the top two candidates—then the Senate's choice would be promoted to president. It's an unlikely but possible scenario.

There Are Other Ways
States
The Electoral College is unique to the national government of the United States. Every state allows its citizens to vote directly for its executives—the governor and lieutenant governor. In fact, because of the one-person/one-vote rule, it's likely that the Supreme Court would declare any mechanism like the Electoral College at the state level unconstitutional.

Other Countries
No other major country has anything like the Electoral College.

The United States
According to opinion polls taken since 1944, as many as 80 percent of Americans want to replace the Electoral College with direct voting. The most straightforward way to do so is by amending the Constitution. Madison called for this process to occur as far back as 1823.

THE ELECTORAL COLLEGE HANDED THE WHITE HOUSE TO THE LESS POPULAR CANDIDATE 3 TIMES AFTER JACKSON

IN 1888

GROVER CLEVELAND GOT **90,000** MORE VOTES THAN BENJAMIN HARRISON, BUT HARRISON WON

IN 2000

AL GORE JR. GOT **500,000** MORE VOTES THAN GEORGE W. BUSH, BUT BUSH WON

IN 2016

HILLARY RODHAM CLINTON GOT **2,800,000** MORE VOTES THAN DONALD J. TRUMP BUT TRUMP WON

was tried was in 1969, when the proposal passed overwhelmingly in the House. President Nixon got on board and a majority of state legislatures said they'd adopt it. However, southern segregationists filibustered and killed the amendment in the Senate.

As a result, most suggestions for making presidential elections more representative of the people's wishes recognize that the Electoral College is here to stay. Instead, they focus on work-arounds. Proposals include the following.

Eliminate winner-take-all. Electors' votes could be allocated proportionately to the citizens' votes. If 52 percent of voters favor a particular candidate, for example, then 52 percent of that state's Electoral College votes would do the same. Or votes could be allocated by congressional district, as they are in Maine and Nebraska, with the statewide winner getting the two bonus votes.

Adopt the National Popular Vote plan. This proposal consists of an agreement among states to cast their

Around six hundred amendments regarding the Electoral College have already been proposed, but they have all been either defeated or abandoned. The most dramatic time this strategy

Electoral College votes for the winner of the popular vote. In order for the National Popular Vote plan to go into effect, states that have a combined total of 270 electoral votes would have to accept it. At that point, the vote count in other states is irrelevant. So far, fourteen states, totaling 189 electoral votes, have joined the compact.

Both of these alternatives pose problems. Proportional voting still gives the advantage to states with low populations because their electoral votes would reflect the boost they get from having two senators. In addition, there's no guarantee that any candidate would win a majority. Furthermore, allocating the vote by congressional district would raise issues related to partisan gerrymandering and who lives in those districts. We certainly would not want that!

It's not clear that enough states will agree to the National Popular Vote plan. Democratic- leaning California, for example, might have to promise to cast its votes for a Republican, or Republican Texas might have to vote for a Democrat. They might find that too hard to swallow—especially if the results were close, if the winner failed to get a majority of the votes, or if there were suspicions that votes were suppressed to tilt the election.

The Story Continues

The Electoral College vote from Florida was so contentious that the decision about who would be inaugurated president on January 20, 2001, was thrown to the Supreme Court.

Two days after the election, Florida's votes were finally counted, but the results were microscopically close: Bush led Gore by only three hundred ballots out of six million cast. Each side challenged the other over whether the tally had been conducted correctly, whether the ballots were confusing, and whether the recount should be done for the whole state or just for certain counties. The process and the arguments carried on for weeks.

There was pressure, however, to

resolve the disputes and pick a winner because of two other mandates. The law says that electors must vote on the first Monday after the second Wednesday in December—in this case, December 18, 2000. Also the Constitution sets January 20 as Inauguration Day.

On December 12, 2000, the Supreme Court ruled that the recount had to end. That decision left Bush the winner in Florida—and, because of the state's Electoral College votes, the winner for the country, even though he didn't get a majority of the votes.

∽ ∾

"...we may never know with complete certainty the identity of the winner of this year's Presidential election."

—Supreme Court Justice John Paul Stevens

∽ ∾

With the court's decision, the Electoral College voted 271 to 266 for Bush.

Did you notice that the number of electoral votes totals only 537, not 538? That's because a faithless elector in the District of Columbia abstained in protest.

PART V
Can the President Really Do That?!

The three-part government the Framers established means that the president shares power with Congress and the federal courts in a variety of ways. This arrangement is known as checks and balances.

In several areas, though, the president has unchecked power and can do just about whatever they please. This section points out problems with two of these areas:

- presidential pardons: the president's ability to grant pardons or lessen the punishment for people who are convicted of or who might have committed a federal crime
- the unitary executive: the president's control over the entire executive branch of the government

The Framers gave these areas less thought and explanation than other issues they grappled with during the Convention. They just weren't as high a priority. This lapse has given presidents the opportunity to make the most of these powers.

CHAPTER 13

Pardon Me?
Presidential Pardons

Stop! Thief!

On June 17, 1972, five men were caught breaking into the headquarters of the Democratic National Committee, which was housed in the Watergate building complex in Washington, DC. They were arrested, and it soon came out that they had been attempting to steal documents and attach bugging devices to the Democrats' telephones. The situation raised alarms not only for the police but also for politicians. One of the burglars was working for CREEP, the Committee for the Re-election of the President—Republican President Richard M. Nixon—in the upcoming November election. But the full details of the robbery did not come out until after the election, which Nixon handily won.

Over the next two years, journalists Bob Woodward and Carl Bernstein of the *Washington Post* investigated the burglary. So did a Senate committee headed by Senator Sam Ervin and Special Prosecutor Archibald Cox for the Department of Justice. During the resulting hearings, testimony revealed that the burglars had been paid hundreds of thousands of dollars to keep quiet about the involvement of CREEP and other high-level officials. Ervin's committee held televised hearings, during which a White House aide, Alexander Butterfield, mentioned that the president recorded all conversations in the Oval Office. Cox demanded the tapes. Nixon refused to release them and then ordered that Attorney General Elliot Richardson fire Cox.

This rash act triggered what was called the Saturday Night Massacre, during which Richardson, as well as Deputy Attorney General William Ruckelshaus, resigned rather than obey Nixon's demand to oust Cox.

The Supreme Court ruled that Nixon had to turn over the tapes. When he finally did so, they confirmed that he not only knew about the burglary but had also attempted to hide it. The cover-up amounted to obstruction of justice, a crime for which a president can be impeached. Oddly, eighteen minutes of the tapes—possibly containing even more incriminating evidence—had somehow been erased. The president tried to defend himself.

છ ૹ

"I am not a crook."

—President Richard M. Nixon

છ ૹ

Meanwhile, the courts found more than a dozen associates of Nixon and members of his staff, including former Attorney General John Mitchell, guilty of various Watergate-related crimes. With criticism from congresspeople and the public swelling, the president recognized that the House of Representatives would probably vote to impeach him, and the Senate would convict him. On August 8, 1974, Nixon chose to resign— the first president to do so.

Vice President Gerald Ford was sworn into office the next day. Six weeks later, saying that Nixon had "suffered enough," Ford granted him a "full, free and absolute pardon" for all crimes he "committed or may have committed" while in the White House.

Meanwhile, Back in 1787

The Framers wanted to balance the powers the president would have with those given to both Congress and the federal courts. It was the job of the court system to determine whether people accused of crimes were guilty and, if so, how they should be punished. One way to limit the influence of the courts would be to let the president pardon guilty parties. The Framers had to decide whether the president could pardon all kinds of crimes and misdeeds or just some. They also had to figure out if the president could act alone or if he needed to get approval from Congress before pardoning someone.

Charles Pinckney of South Carolina proposed that the chief executive have the same pardon power that British monarchs traditionally held—the ability to pardon in all cases. Pinckney made an exception, though, for impeachment of any officer.

George Mason of Virginia objected, pointing out that the president might hire someone to carry out a crime and then pardon the perpetrator to save his own skin. Or, if he granted a pardon before the wrongdoer went to trial, the criminal might never be revealed.

Such an act would be especially damaging if the president committed treason, because his treachery might remain hidden. James Wilson of Pennsylvania assured Mason that, if that happened, Congress would surely find out and impeach and prosecute the president. Others at the convention argued that the Senate should have the right to approve a presidential pardon.

Ultimately, the Framers decided that Pinckney had it right. The Pardon Clause, as Article II, Section 2 is known, grants the president wide-open powers to pardon, except when impeachment is involved, without anybody else's say-so. The president can also commute a sentence, meaning shorten it.

෨ ෧

"The President...shall have the Power to grant Reprieves and Pardons for Offences against the United States, except in Cases of Impeachment."

—Article II, Section 2

෨ ෧

Writing the next year in *The Federalist*, Alexander Hamilton explained his support for giving the president broad powers to pardon. One reason was compassion. Judges and juries make mistakes, after all. Also, some people justly convicted of crimes genuinely repent and beg forgiveness. In such cases, the president should be able to dispense "the mercy of government."

Just as important, Hamilton argued, was the president's right to pardon even traitors if doing so would "restore the tranquility of the commonwealth" and heal old political wounds. The first three presidents exercised that right.

In 1795, George Washington pardoned grain farmers in western Pennsylvania who had been sentenced to death for taking up arms against US tax collectors during the Whiskey Rebellion. John Adams issued an amnesty in 1800 for other tax resisters convicted of treason during Fries's Rebellion. (Amnesty is the term sometimes used for pardons when lots of people are involved.) And the following year, Thomas Jefferson pardoned prisoners convicted of disobeying the Alien and Sedition Acts because he considered these laws unconstitutional.

So What's the Big Problem?

The president's power to grant pardons is so broad that they can erase a criminal conviction as if it had never happened, regardless of the nature of the crime or the rationale for the pardon.

Pardoning behavior that is possibly traitorous is both allowed and controversial. During the Civil War, Vice President Andrew Johnson, a Democrat, referred to secessionists, saying, "The traitors must be impoverished." But when he became president after the assassination of Abraham Lincoln, Johnson granted "amnesty and pardon" to tens of thousands of Confederates.

He did so partly because he believed in white supremacy—the view that white people are better than black people and should continue to oversee them. Also, he said he wanted to "fully restore confidence and fraternal feeling among the whole people." Americans who agreed with the old Johnson were appalled.

On President Jimmy Carter's second day in office in 1977, he pardoned as many as two hundred thousand young American men who had fled to Canada and other countries between 1964 and 1973 in order to avoid being drafted into the armed forces. These men believed the war in Vietnam was immoral, but many people viewed them as traitors. The reason Carter gave for his action was "to heal our country." However, the American Legion, a veterans' organization, complained that it would divide the country instead. Reactions around the country ranged from relief to outrage.

Presidents can give pardons in several ways and for many reasons and never have to explain them. Bill Clinton cleared his brother of drug charges, though such actions on behalf of family members are unusual. President Ronald Reagan pardoned Junior Johnson, a professional sports car racer who

HOW TO GET A GET-OUT-OF-JAIL-FREE CARD

There are two routes to requesting a pardon from the president. Typically, wrongdoers submit a petition to the Office of Pardon Attorney at the Department of Justice. Then, they follow a multistep process, including a five-year waiting period.

Or, wrongdoers can ask someone who knows the president to lobby for a pardon on their behalf. This route has become more common under President Donald J. Trump. Either way, the petitioner might get good news from the president—or no response at all.

had committed a felony by operating a moonshine still.

President Trump commuted—that is, shortened—the sentence of Alice Marie Johnson, who was serving life in prison for a nonviolent drug offense. The offense was not erased but she was released from jail. Trump gave his reason in a prepared statement: "those who have paid their debt to society…deserve a second chance." He also pardoned Sheriff Joe Arpaio of Maricopa County, Arizona, who had been convicted of contempt of court for using racist practices against Mexican-Americans. Arpaio was pardoned before he had been jailed or paid his debt to society.

Furthermore, presidents can pardon someone who has not even been indicted, tried, or convicted of anything. This was how President Ford handled Nixon's situation, which allowed the disgraced former president to avoid even the prospect of a trial.

It turns out that George Mason had a good point when he wondered if the president might use the pardon power preemptively to protect himself. On December 24, 1992, President George H. W. Bush pardoned people who had participated in a scandal called the Iran-Contra Affair. In an effort to support rebels in Nicaragua and secure the release of American hostages held in Lebanon, government officials secretly

---

PARDON? NO, THANKS.

In 1830, George Wilson and James Porter were convicted of robbing the US mail and assaulting the stagecoach driver. The two were sentenced to death, and Porter was executed. President Andrew Jackson pardoned Wilson, commuting his punishment to prison time. Remarkably, Wilson responded that he "did not wish in any manner to avail himself to avoid sentence." The Supreme Court decided that a presidential pardon is a gift, which the recipient can refuse to accept. Wilson, too, was executed.

---

sold missiles to Iran. In exchange, Iran freed the hostages and the United States sent the money earned from the arms sales to the rebels.

There were at least two problems with this arrangement. First, the United States had a trade embargo with Iran; the government wasn't supposed to sell them anything, much less arms. Secondly, Congress had barred shipping cash or other resources to Nicaraguan insurgents. Bush had been vice president when both transactions were made and carried out. Many people viewed his Christmas Eve pardons, just weeks before he would be leaving office, as an attempt to protect himself. Since all of the participants were pardoned, they were not under pressure to offer evidence about Bush's possible role in the illegal arrangements.

An even more dramatic example arose during Watergate, when Americans wondered whether President Nixon would try to pardon himself. The Department of Justice issued a legal opinion saying that he could not since "no person can be the judge of his own case." But that was only one opinion, and some lawyers interpret the wide-open language of the Pardon Clause to allow the possibility of self-pardon.

This question arose again during Trump's presidency. Robert Mueller, a special prosecutor, looked into the possibility that Russia had been involved in Trump's campaign during the 2016 election. Some of the president's

OFF AND RUNNING

Most people who receive a pardon are reinstated into society. John C. Frémont did even better. After President James K. Polk gave him a pardon for committing mutiny, he ran as the Republican candidate for president in 1856.

actions seemed to suggest he was obstructing justice by interfering with the investigation.

President Trump can pardon anyone who was caught up in the inquiry or found guilty. He also declared that he could pardon himself—though he said that he wouldn't need to because he'd done nothing wrong. If he did, though, the question would be whether James Wilson was right. Would Congress consider a president's self-pardon to be such an abuse of power that it would warrant impeachment? No one knows the answer, and it remains unclear whether there are any limits on the president's pardon power other than impeachment.

There Are Other Ways

States

Every state has adopted legislation regarding procedures for pardons. More than half require that the judge who sentenced the person applying be allowed to comment on whether the applicant deserves the pardon. After that, the power to grant a pardon varies from state to state.

• Twenty-nine states allow their governors to grant pardons. In most of these states—including Alaska, California, Hawaii, New York, North Carolina, Ohio, and West Virginia—an advisory board makes recommendations to the governor, though the executive is not bound to accept them.

• Another nine states—including Connecticut, Georgia, Idaho, South Carolina, and Utah—appoint a clemency board, such as a Board of Pardons and Parole, to make the decisions.

• The remaining twelve states—including Arizona, Florida, Louisiana, Montana, and Texas—divide the power between the governor and a board.

BY THE POWER VESTED IN ME, I PARDON MYSELF

In 1856, Isaac Stevens, the territorial governor of the Pacific Northwest, ordered farmers who had married Native Americans to leave the area. When the court system investigated whether the order was legal, Stevens closed them down, declared martial law, and had the judges arrested. Another court then fined him for contempt. To avoid the punishment, he pardoned himself.

No state has specified whether governors can pardon themselves.

Other Countries

The presidents of France and Germany can grant pardons, as in the United States. However, only the legislature in Germany can grant amnesty to a group of people. The British monarch can grant pardons but she does so on the advice of the Home Secretary.

Unlike the arrangement in the United States, the Parole Board of

Canada makes the decision, and a Canadian pardon does not erase the original conviction. In Japan, the Cabinet does the job.

The Israeli president grants pardons based on recommendations by the Minister of Justice. In honor of its seventieth anniversary as a country in 2018, President Reuven Rivlin of Israel expanded the number of pardons "for the sake of mercy and kindness."

The United States

Americans might benefit from a more orderly process for presidential pardons given to individuals for reasons of mercy. This could include review and recommendations by the Department of Justice or an independent board. The right to bestow amnesties on a number of people in order to preserve domestic tranquility could be retained by the president as would pardons given for political reasons.

The Story Continues

After resigning, Nixon returned to his home in California. In his speech to Congress upon taking the oath of office, Ford declared, "Our long national nightmare is over." However, he was widely criticized for pardoning Nixon, and he lost his race for election in 1976. After Ford died in 2006, though, many editorialists suggested that he had done the right thing. It was enough that Nixon was forced to resign, they suggested; jailing a former president would not have contributed to national healing.

CHAPTER 14

"You're Hired! (Maybe.) You're Fired!"
The Unitary Executive

Breaking News!

At 2:00 p.m. on May 9, 2017, James B. Comey, director of the Federal Bureau of Investigation, stood at a lectern giving a speech to agents at a field office in Los Angeles. Behind him, a television screen set to the local ABC station started flashing an alert. A newscaster announced, "Breaking news that no one saw coming today!… President Trump has informed FBI director James Comey that he has been terminated and removed from office."

That was certainly news to the suddenly-former director, who had not been informed of any such thing. In fact, Comey laughed, assuming the announcement was a prank—until his aides checked messages on their telephones and told him the story was true.

At first, President Donald J. Trump said that his reason for this dramatic action was Comey's mishandling of investigations into Hillary Rodham Clinton's use of a private email server while she was secretary of state. The director had concluded that she had behaved irresponsibly, but there was not sufficient reason to charge her with a crime. Trump disagreed.

It soon came out, however, that Trump probably had another reason to let Comey go. The FBI had also started looking into efforts by the Russian government to interfere with the 2016 presidential election. And, the inquiry included possible communications between Russians and some Trump campaign staffers and family members. The president called allegations of such links "a made-up story" and told Comey in his termination letter, "you are not able to effectively lead the Bureau."

A Republican appointed by President Barack Obama to head the FBI in 2013, Comey had served in the Department of Justice under President George W. Bush. Congress had established a ten-year term to protect the FBI director from political pressure. Since only one director had ever been fired, Comey anticipated that he would lead the FBI for another six years.

On the other hand, he was aware that his relationship with Trump had deteriorated over the previous months. After all, he hadn't even responded when the president suggested that he stop investigating contacts between Russia and the White House's national security advisor, Michael Flynn. Soon, Trump talked openly of firing Comey, although his aides advised him not to because it would look suspicious if he did. Referring to the director as a

"nutjob," Trump carried out his threat anyway.

Comey immediately returned to Washington, DC, to clean out his desk.

Meanwhile, Back in 1787 (and 1789)

Within two weeks of getting to work, the Framers agreed that the country should have only one president at a time. His job would be to implement whatever laws got passed. Of course, he'd need helpers, called officers, to execute his plans. But who should select the officers—the president or the legislature?

The Framers didn't answer that question for another three months. First, they had to decide what powers each branch of the government should have and how those powers should check and balance each other.

Alexander Hamilton of New York believed the Senate should have a say in choosing the key players in the executive branch. If the president had sole power over appointments, he might choose people "personally allied to him," such as relatives, buddies, or business partners who would do whatever he demanded. Since the Senate, on the other hand, would be composed of "independent and public-spirited men," they would ensure that the president picked worthy staff committed to what's best for the public.

The Framers put together a combination of these ideas. They gave the president the ability to nominate those who work for him. But, high-ranking officials couldn't be appointed without "the advice and consent of the Senate." In addition, Congress would decide what offices to establish and presume the president would fill them.

❧ ❧

The President shall...nominate and, by and with the Advice and Consent of the Senate, shall appoint... Officers of the United States, whose Appointments are not herein otherwise provided for, and which shall be established by Law: but the Congress may by Law vest the Appointment of such inferior Officers, as they think proper, in the President alone...or in the Heads of Departments.

—Article II, Section 2

❧ ❧

Two days after agreeing that power over the most important appointments should be shared between the executive and legislative branches, the Framers signed their Constitution and went home. In their rush to get out the door, though, they neglected to talk about the opposite situation—how could the president dismiss someone he had appointed? Could he fire the person himself? Or, did the Senate have to approve the removal?

The Constitution doesn't say. So in 1789, during a crisis early in George Washington's first term, Congress made the decision that the Framers had ignored.

One of the most urgent duties of the First United States Congress was to establish departments to help run the government. The heads of these departments would become the president's cabinet. As to appointing them, Washington said, "I have no conception of a more delicate task than that which is imposed by the Constitution on the executive."

The House of Representatives considered a bill creating the Department of Foreign Affairs; today, it's called the State Department. The bill said the department was to be led by a secretary who would be "removable from office by the President of the United States." This simple language, with no mention of the Senate, stirred up a furor in both houses that lasted for a week.

One side argued that since the Senate was involved in appointments, it should approve or disapprove dismissals as well. If the president acted on his own, Representative Alexander White of Virginia said, he might cause a "violent...revolution in the officers of the Government." That is, there would be a revolving door of senior staffers.

James Madison, another Virginian, on the other hand, confidently predicted that the Electoral College would

guarantee the selection of presidents so upstanding they wouldn't fire someone without a good reason.

ॐ ॐ

"...the instances will be very rare in which an unworthy man will...[become] President of the United States."

—James Madison

ॐ ॐ

The issue at stake was the power of the presidency versus the power of the legislature. The fifty-nine members of the House and twenty senators took it very seriously. Representative Richard Bland Lee, also of Virginia, declared that the outcome would determine "the future happiness or misery of the people of America."

The House voted to let the president alone remove appointees. The Senate tied, ten to ten. As president of the Senate, Vice President John Adams broke the tie in a way that surely pleased his boss, President Washington. From then on, with a brief exception, the president has had the sole right to fire officials in the executive branch.

So, What's the Big Problem?

This section of the Constitution raises two alarms. The Framers were aware of one: a president might fire someone to protect himself rather than the country, and Congress would be stymied. The other one has arisen over the last two hundred and thirty years: the executive branch has ballooned enormously.

Like the chief executive officer of a business, the president is the CEO of the executive branch of the government. Just as the head of a business can hire and fire employees, presidents have the right to hire—with the Senate's approval—high-level officials to undertake their policies. And, they can get rid of someone who doesn't do a good job or who undermines them. (Laws, though, protect employees from being fired because of their race, gender, or age.)

This system of an executive branch led by a single person at the top who oversees major employees below is called a "unitary executive." Because the executive chooses the underlings and doesn't have to get permission before firing them, the president has a lot of power.

In 1867, President Andrew Johnson feuded with his Secretary of War, Edwin Stanton, over Reconstruction policies. Concerned that Johnson would get rid of Stanton, the Thirty-ninth Congress undid the decision of the First Congress by passing the Tenure of Office Act. This law required the president to get

Senate approval before kicking out certain officeholders. Johnson fired Stanton anyway, so the House moved to impeach the president. Johnson was saved by one vote in the Senate. The act, which many lawyers consider unconstitutional to start out with, was repealed in 1887.

More recently, on the hiring side, many Americans were appalled when President John F. Kennedy nominated Robert F. Kennedy—his brother!—for attorney general. As head of the Department of Justice, the AG is the president's main legal advisor and the country's chief law enforcer. And, people worried about what Bobby would let John get away with. This was the situation Hamilton feared. An anti-nepotism law, later passed by Congress, bars officials from hiring relatives to work in the agency they oversee.

On the firing side, President Jimmy Carter booted four cabinet secretaries all at once. President Richard M. Nixon demanded letters of resignation from his entire cabinet at the beginning of his second term, though he allowed most of

CIVIL SERVICE

Most government employees are civil servants, meaning that they are hired by an agency or department rather than elected by voters or appointed by officeholders. They cannot be fired for political reasons or let go when a new administration takes over.

them to stay. This was Representative White's revolving-door concern.

Less than a year after Trump announced Comey's ouster through a television news program, he ejected his secretary of state, Rex Tillerson, by a tweet. He later fired Attorney General Jeff Sessions.

On the other hand, Trump could not directly fire Robert Mueller, the special prosecutor who investigated links between Russians and the president's staff and family. Mueller was appointed by Deputy Attorney General Rod Rosenstein after Sessions recused himself—that is, he took himself off the case—when it came out that he, too, had communicated with Russians during the presidential campaign. DOJ

DECIDER-IN-CHIEF

In 2006, military leaders urged President George W. Bush to replace Secretary of Defense Donald Rumsfeld. In response, Bush stated, "I'm the decider, and I decide what is best."

rules said that only Rosenstein could let Mueller go.

But what if Trump had ordered Rosenstein to get rid of Mueller, before the Deputy AG resigned in 2019, in order to halt the investigation? If he refused, the president could have replaced him with someone who would comply with his demand. That would be similar to Nixon's Saturday Night Massacre. The president chose not to fire Rosenstein, partly because Republican senators warned the president that would be politically disastrous.

In addition to the offices that require Senate confirmation, Congress has created more than three hundred other positions within the White House—for example, the press secretary—that the president can fill without their approval.

The most important of these may be the National Security Advisor, who counsels the president on foreign policy. Unlike the secretary of state, who also advises and carries out foreign policy, the NSA reports only to the person in the Oval Office. NSAs never have to explain or even reveal their actions to Congress or the public.

Nixon's NSA, Henry Kissinger, upended US policy with China by secretly arranging a meeting between his boss and Chairman Mao Tse Tung in Beijing in 1972. Their face-to-face talk was path-breaking but the people's elected lawmakers had been left in the dark. So was Secretary of State William Rogers.

These unconfirmable positions are just one way the executive branch has swelled since 1789. During Washington's two terms, Congress authorized four cabinet departments and a couple of hundred positions to staff them.

Trump, on the other hand, oversees fifteen cabinet members, more than one hundred federal agencies, and over three million employees. Most work in the Department of Defense. The Senate is charged with confirming—or rejecting—about 1,200 high-ranking officials once they are nominated. The president also appoints hundreds of others and can dismiss almost all of them.

This arrangement gives modern-day presidents a lot of sway. We must hope that, as Madison suggested, they are worthy of the job.

There are Other Ways

States

Most states do not have a unitary executive. Top officials other than the governor are elected or appointed separately, so the governor does not hire and cannot fire them. This system has been called an "unbundled executive."

New Jersey is the only state whose governor appoints almost all executive offices but, even there, the governor cannot fire the attorney general. At the other extreme, Texas's governor appoints only the secretary of state. Voter's select other offices, including the State Board of Education and the Railroad Commission, which oversees oil and gas policies.

In forty-three states, the people elect their attorney general. In three others, that person is elected by the state legislature. Tennessee's Supreme Court appoints its AG. Only Alaska, Hawaii, New Hampshire, New Jersey, and Wyoming allow the governor to appoint that official.

The lieutenant governor is like the vice president of a state. But while the president chooses their running mate, only eighteen states allow the gubernatorial candidate to pick the lieutenant governor. These include California, Florida, and North and South Dakota. In seventeen states, including Alabama, Delaware, Rhode Island, and Texas, these two positions are elected entirely separately. The legislatures in Tennessee and West Virginia vote for the second in command.

Other Countries

Heads of government in parliamentary systems, such as the prime minister in Britain and the chancellor of Germany, have great powers to hire and fire their cabinet ministers. Nevertheless, these heads have to negotiate with the ministers to put together and hold onto their government.

The United States

The Senate barely has time to consider the large number of the president's nominees who are already under its control, let alone to ponder firing them. So, Congress's decision of 1789 continues to make sense. The exception, however, might be the attorney general and other key law enforcement personnel, including the head of the FBI. Some people might include the secretaries of Defense and Treasury in this list as well. The president's ability to summarily dismiss these officers can be dangerous.

The number and importance of other presidential appointees within the White House has expanded. Perhaps they should be confirmable as well. More importantly, Congress should have authority to question them, holding them publicly accountable for their advice and actions, just as it does other high-level officers who must be confirmed by the Senate.

The Story Continues

President Trump was furious at Sessions, probably because he had counted on the AG to stifle the probe into his staff's contacts with Russians. He fired Sessions in 2018 and nominated William Barr to the post; the Senate confirmed Barr in 2019.

❧ ❧

"At your request, I am submitting my resignation."
—Former Attorney General Jeff Sessions

❧ ❧

Meanwhile, Trump declined to nominate hundreds of the 1,200 positions that Congress established to run the government. Less than half of those at the Department of Justice were filled and the State department was described as empty. He blamed Democrats. James Comey wrote a book criticizing President Trump's leadership.

PART VI
Who's Running America?

Accidents happen. So do acts of terrorism. Our Constitution, however, doesn't make provisions for such events if they result in a need to replace our national leadership. It lays out guidelines for succession should a president die in office, but it doesn't cover other important details.

The fault lines we address in this section deal with potentially frightening situations. Some are more likely to occur than others, though none is impossible. In all cases, the Constitution could fail us just when we need it most.

We look at what happens when

- representatives and senators are unable to finish their terms;
- the president is unable to complete her or his term—and might not realize it; and
- a new president has to deal with a mess that the outgoing president created just before leaving office.

CHAPTER 15

Knock Knock. Is Anybody There?
Continuity in Government

"Call the Authorities"

Tom Burnett reached Newark, New Jersey's International Airport early enough on the morning of September 11, 2001, to nab a seat on a morning United Airlines flight to San Francisco. He'd get home earlier than he'd planned.

At about the same time, Representative Jim Matheson, a Democrat from Utah, was meeting with his staff at the Capitol to discuss an upcoming Budget Committee meeting.

Burnett's plane pulled away from the gate only a minute behind schedule. Then, with heavy traffic at the airport, UA 93 sat on the tarmac for nearly forty more minutes before it finally became airborne at 8:42 a.m.

At about 8:45, Matheson walked into a windowless conference room in the House Office Building.

Between 9:24 and 9:28 a.m., Burnett watched four passengers tie red bandannas around their heads, stab and kill a flight attendant and the man sitting directly behind him, and rush at the cockpit door. Then he saw both pilots sprawled in pools of blood just outside the cockpit and felt the plane plummet seven hundred feet.

As soon as the Budget Committee concluded its business, Matheson and his staff walked back to his office where he held a meet and greet with constituents.

Burnett called his wife, Deena. "I'm

on an airplane that's been hijacked," he quietly explained. "Call the authorities."

When Matheson emerged from his meeting, he learned that two jets had dive-bombed into the World Trade Center buildings in New York City. A security guard hurried down the hall calling, "Evacuate the building! Evacuate the building!"

As the hijacker-pilot roller-coastered the plane thousands of vertical feet, Burnett again called Deena, who told him about other hijacked flights that had crashed into buildings in New York. "Oh my gosh!" he exclaimed. "It's a suicide mission."

Matheson and most of his assistants filed out of their office building. His remaining staff members were still in the Capitol Rotunda, giving constituents a tour.

Burnett and other passengers tried to take control of the cockpit. They didn't succeed, but their attempts convinced the hijackers that they couldn't stay aloft long enough to reach their target. Just after 10:00 a.m., the flyers spun the jet upside-down and torpedoed it into the ground near Shanksville, Pennsylvania.

Matheson and his staff convened at his apartment about three blocks from the Capitol.

As Burnett had figured out, UA 93 was on a murder-suicide mission. The target was most likely the United States Capitol Complex, which held Matheson's—and every other representative's and senator's—office and sat only twenty minutes' flying time from Shanksville.

Meanwhile, Back in 1787 (and 1913)...

The Framers worried that representatives who lived nearest the capital city might take advantage of those who lived farther away and could not show up as often. So they included the requirement that a quorum—a majority, one half of the members plus one more—be present to conduct business.

❧ ❧

"...a Majority of each [of the House and Senate] shall constitute a Quorum to do Business."

—Article I, Section 5

❧ ❧

But what if vacancies emerged because representatives or senators died in office or resigned for some reason? The Framers had spent so much time and energy disagreeing with each other about the makeup and duties of Congress, they hardly talked at all about how to fill a vacancy.

They wanted to make sure that replacements for members of the House of Representatives would be elected by their constituents no matter what. The House was envisioned as "the people's branch," so the Framers could not conceive of circumstances under which a congressman should be appointed. Every representative should run the gauntlet of a popular election. As a result, the Constitution directs the governor of a missing representative's state to call a special election in the district.

❧ ❧

"When vacancies happen in the Representation [the House of Representatives] from any State, the Executive Authority thereof shall issue Writs of Election to fill such Vacancies."

—Article I, Section 2

❧ ❧

The Senate was treated differently. At that time, senators were not elected by the public; they were appointed by state legislatures. So, with little discussion, the Framers decided that state legislatures should replace absent senators as long as they were in session. When legislatures were in recess, the governor would name new senators to take the place of those who left office before their terms were up. The goal was to fill vacancies quickly, possibly because senators had more important responsibilities than representatives did, including confirming presidential appointments and ratifying treaties. Also, that body was smaller, so vacancies would be more noticeable.

❧ ❧

"The Senate of the United States shall be composed of two Senators from each State, chosen by the Legislature thereof... and if Vacancies happen by Resignation, or otherwise, during the Recess of the Legislature of any State, the Executive thereof may make temporary Appointments until the next Meeting of the Legislature, which shall then fill such Vacancies."

—Article I, Section 3

❧ ❧

This arrangement changed when the Seventeenth Amendment was ratified in 1913. Senators would no longer be appointed by state legislatures; they would be elected by the people. And so the amendment added that legislatures could give the governor the ability to call for another election to replace senators. Meanwhile, governors could temporarily fill the empty spot.

❧ ❧

"When vacancies happen in the representation of any State in the Senate, the executive authority of such State shall issue writs of election to fill such vacancies: *Provided*, That the legislature of any State may empower the executive thereof to make temporary appointments until the people fill the vacancies by election as the legislature may direct."

—Seventeenth Amendment

❧ ❧

With rare exceptions, states always have senators representing them, whether elected or appointed by governors. They do not necessarily have a full delegation of representatives, however, if there is a lag between a congressperson's departure and the election of a new one.

APPOINT ME!
I MEAN, VOTE FOR ME.

Problems cropped up with the system of state legislatures appointing senators. Some legislatures failed to agree on whom to appoint. Delaware, for instance, sent only one senator to Congress between 1899 and 1903. Furthermore, some senators bought their seats by paying off corrupt state legislators.

Incensed, folks—especially out West—wanted to pick their senators instead of relying on state legislatures to do so. So, many states started holding straw elections in which Senate wannabes could compete with one another. Candidates who ran for their state legislatures promised to honor the results of these competitions by voting for the winner when the legislature named its US senators.

Public pressure grew to strip states of the power to appoint senators. Between 1893 and 1908, two-thirds of the House of Representatives approved an amendment calling for direct election of senators by the people. Every proposal died in the Senate.

The situation finally got the senators' attention in 1912, when twenty-seven states passed petitions calling for a second Constitutional Convention. With support from only four more states, a Constitutional Convention would have happened. The Senate gave in and agreed to the Seventeenth Amendment, which the states quickly ratified.

So What's the Big Problem?

The American government needs to continue to function even—and especially—when a large number of its elected officials are killed or incapacitated. This issue is called continuity in government. The Constitution's mechanisms for replacing politicians on a wholesale basis, in case of a widespread emergency, are unwieldy, inefficient, and dysfunctional.

What if UA 93 had not been delayed on the ground for forty minutes? What if Burnett's cell phone couldn't grab a signal? What if the passengers hadn't tried to wrest the plane from the hijackers? Fortunately, for the sake of over a thousand representatives, senators, and staffers, we didn't find out what might have happened, since UA 93 didn't hit the Capitol.

Unfortunately, our enemies don't need to commandeer a jetliner to cause such a catastrophe. In 2012, a physicist from Massachusetts tried to fly model planes packed with grenades and what he believed were plastic explosives into government buildings. Five years later, an angry guy with a military style rifle and a handgun fired fifty rounds of ammunition at congressmen playing baseball.

Drones might be able to accomplish the same result as hijackers. So could powdered or gaseous poisons or engineered viruses. These are all terrorist acts.

Natural disasters or diseases dispersed by mosquitoes or pigs could also wipe out many government officials—along with much of the rest of us. More people died in the influenza epidemic in 1919 than during World War I.

ॐ ॐ

"Natural epidemics can be extremely large. Intentionally caused epidemics, bioterrorism, would be the largest of all."

—Bill Gates

ॐ ॐ

It might sound simple enough for a governor to call for an election to replace a member of the House of Representatives. Elections occur all the time. But even special elections have to follow normal procedures, which vary from state to state.

First, the election has to be scheduled, following state law.

Both major political parties (and smaller third parties, if there are any) need to

- find people who want to run;
- raise money;
- give candidates a chance to campaign;
- hold primary elections, caucuses, or conventions to reduce the number of candidates to one per party;

MEMBERS OF CONGRESS MISSING IN ACTION

In all, 301 senators and 817 members of the House have died in office—three of them between their election and swearing-in ceremony. An additional twenty have been expelled.

Spencer Darwin Pettis, the first member of Congress killed in office, died in a duel in 1831 after he criticized the president of the Bank of the United States. The banker's brother, Thomas Biddle, took offense and challenged Pettis. They squared off on Bloody Island in the Mississippi River. Biddle was so nearsighted that he chose to shoot pistols at short range—so short a range that the shooters killed each other.

Elected officials also leave office for reasons other than death and then need to be replaced. Here are a few examples.

- Senators John F. Kennedy and Barack Obama moved into the White House as presidents.
- Senators Hillary Rodham Clinton and John Kerry both became Secretaries of State under President Obama, and several other senators also joined his administration.
- President Donald J. Trump named Alabama Senator Jeff Sessions to serve as the US Attorney General, Kansas Representative Mike Pompeo to head the Central Intelligence Agency, Montana Representative Ryan Zinke to be Secretary of the Interior, and Georgia Representative Tom Price to head the Department of Health and Human Services.

- hold a runoff primary if no one wins enough votes;
- encourage voters to get to the polls;
- and, finally, hold the election.

This process can take as little as two months or up to six months.

The missing representative's staff members can carry out jobs like answering mail and phone calls from constituents. But no one else besides the representatives can hold committee hearings or vote on bills. The constituents back home are literally unrepresented.

The constitutional process to replace a senator can take even longer than for a House member since the election is statewide, not just within a single congressional district.

Thirty-six governors are allowed to appoint an interim senator, which can occur overnight. That person keeps the post until the next regular election. Some states limit the governor's freedom to choose by requiring, for example, that the successor be from the same party as the former senator.

Fourteen states require a special election to fill an empty Senate seat. In nine states the governor can name an interim appointee. Five states—North Dakota, Oklahoma, Oregon, Rhode Island, and Wisconsin—require waiting for the special election because they believe that all members of Congress should be elected and not appointed. The seat remains vacant until then.

The system works fairly smoothly following a senator's death or resignation in most states. But what if that

> **TO PASS A LAW, YOU NEED A MAJORITY OF A MAJORITY!**
>
> A quorum = the number of people required to take action; in this case, it's a majority
>
> Enough people in Congress to pass a law = a majority of a quorum

person remains in office, yet is unable to serve because of a severe disability? Here's where the drawback to the requirement for a quorum arises.

Generally it makes sense for political bodies and organizations to agree to binding decisions only when a majority of the members are present. This part of the Constitution, though—Article I, Section 5—is fuzzy about what quorum means.

Congress is composed of 100 senators and 435 representatives. If "a Majority of each" means a majority of each body—that is, of the full House and Senate—here's a possible scenario. If 50 senators or 218 representatives are alive but unable to appear on the floor for a vote because of a disaster, there would not be enough people to make a quorum. In that case, Congress would not have enough members to pass legislation. The government would come to a standstill.

But if "a Majority of each" means a majority of those congresspeople who remain *alive* and are able to get to work, the scenario is entirely different. If, say, 39 senators and 199 representatives are able to show up after a calamity, a quorum would be 20 senators plus 100 representatives. And a majority of that quorum—that is, 11 senators and 51 representatives—could pass or defeat laws for the entire country.

"Alive *and* able to get to work"

would be more useful but we don't know for sure if this is how "a Majority of each" would be defined.

Imagine the truly worst-case scenario: If only three representatives in the House emerge from a catastrophe, then two of them could pass whatever bills they want. The replacements for the remaining 432 members could not be elected for a bare minimum of two months.

If only a few senators survive a disaster, governors in most states could quickly appoint others to replace those who died. This would not be the case if there are many survivors who are injured and left immobilized, intellectually impaired, or comatose.

The Constitution does not say anything about incapacity or disability. Therefore it provides no way either for governors to appoint or for voters to elect new senators to take the place of those who don't or can't resign. Regardless of the extent of any disabilities, senators keep their seats until they

HOUSE OF REPRESENTATIVES	SENATE
IF **199** SURVIVE	IF **39** SURVIVE
100 = QUORUM	**20** = QUORUM
51 = NEEDED TO PASS LAWS	**11** = NEEDED TO PASS LAWS

voluntarily leave office. So we could be stuck with senators who can't function and who can't be replaced.

A doomsday scenario would be a time of great crisis in our country. Important decisions would need to be made quickly. Yet hundreds of millions of Americans could be unrepresented in Congress. Would they accept the binding decisions made by a very small group of legislators?

On the morning of September 11, 2001, congresspeople were scattered throughout the Capitol building. It is impossible to know how many might have been killed or maimed had UA 93 slammed into the building. That afternoon a vote was scheduled; most members would have congregated on the floor. A hit during such a time could have been cataclysmic.

Had the hijackers undertaken their mission five days earlier, they might have wiped out the entire Congress, along with the vice president and the cabinet, all of whom were assembled to

PROJECT GREEK ISLAND

During the 1950s, the federal government ran a top secret bunker called Project Greek Island underneath The Greenbrier, a fancy resort in West Virginia. Its purpose was to house Congress in case of nuclear attack. Members were to sleep in dormitories, with nameplates on their bunk beds. The facility was decommissioned after a reporter let out word about it in 1993. It is now a tourist site.

hear an address by Mexico's President Vicente Fox.

During each State of the Union address, almost all of the chief figures in the federal government assemble at the Capitol to hear the president speak. One cabinet member is ordered *not* to attend so that someone can step into the presidency should disaster strike. But she or he wouldn't be able to accomplish much with no other elected or appointed officials to carry out their jobs.

"I CAN'T BREATHE!"

On 9/11, Vice President Dick Cheney and some officials were bustled into a bunker in the White House. Other officials didn't know where to go. And even many in the bunker were kicked out when the oxygen supply sank to a dangerously low level.

Thereafter, President George W. Bush ordered the Federal Emergency Management Agency (FEMA) to develop a plan to transport government leaders to bunkers in case of another attack. FEMA ran exercises called TOPOFF (for Top Officials) but the computers and other equipment became obsolete.

There Are Other Ways—Maybe

States

Few, if any, governments have tackled the enormity of this situation—possibly because it's too unpleasant to think about—and none has needed to. Some of them, though, have basic provisions in place.

When a vacancy occurs in the California legislature, the governor is required to call for an election to fill it immediately. But that doesn't address a potential wholesale loss of members.

Other Countries

Few countries have policies to address such situations. The French and South African constitutions authorize national legislation to provide ways of filling vacancies; however, the legislatures have not passed appropriate laws.

The United States

The Constitution would have to be amended to change procedures for filling vacancies. Perhaps it could be a simple amendment directing Congress to pass a law on a process to replace its members, as in France and South Africa.

From the end of World War II in 1945 through the Cuban Missile Crisis in 1962 and through the Cold War, many Americans were terrified that the Soviet Union might detonate nuclear weapons in Washington, DC. During that time, Congress proposed more than thirty constitutional amendments that laid out ways to fill seats quickly in the House of Representatives. Most of these allowed governors to make interim appointments. Three proposals passed the Senate by wide margins. The House, however, did not take action on any possible measures to replace itself.

The Story Continues

After 9/11, nearly a dozen additional amendments were introduced to resolve issues of continuity in government. Congress held hearings at which experts, including an author of this book, testified. Consultants wrote reports. Legislation was introduced and voted upon. All to no avail; no plan was adopted.

The House of Representatives did pass a bill that would require expedited elections in case more than a hundred members are killed, but the bill did not address disabled members. Nor did it move through the Senate.

Other suggestions have included interim appointments by governors or by legislatures. Details in various proposals, such as the number of deceased officials that would trigger replacement and the length of time the replacements would serve, are all at odds with each other.

CHAPTER 16

Is There a Leader in the Room?
Presidential Succession

"Who's Minding the Store?"

President Ronald Reagan waved to admirers and reporters as he strolled out of the Washington Hilton Hotel on March 31, 1981, only two months after his inauguration. He'd just given a speech, and his audience of labor union leaders wasn't happy with his plan to cut the federal budget, which could threaten their jobs. Nevertheless, he was generally a popular president.

Just before Reagan reached his limousine, six loud shots cracked, and the pungent scent of sulfur pulsed through the air, breaking the calm of the damp, unusually warm afternoon. Stunned Secret Service agents grabbed their guns and swiveled, looking for the shooter. A disgruntled bystander in the crowd of

admirers? A camera operator? Someone hiding around the corner? No, a young man standing amid reporters about ten feet from the president.

Agents surrounded him and pinned him against the building. "Get him out of here!" one shouted. They carried the shooter to a police cruiser but couldn't open the door and had to find another one.

Jerry Parr, the Special Agent in charge of the Presidential Protection Division, hurled himself into the president, bending him over, and shoved him into the limousine, which sped off toward the White House. Seeing Reagan sitting up in the back seat, witnesses assumed that he remained unhurt. Moments later, Parr spotted the president spitting up blood. The car swerved and raced to George Washington University Hospital.

The car pulled up to the emergency room entrance and Reagan stepped out, hitched up his pants, buttoned his suit jacket, and walked to the door—where he fainted. A .22 caliber bullet had struck his seventh rib an inch from his heart and penetrated his left lung, collapsing it. First Lady Nancy Reagan was rushed to the hospital just before he was wheeled into surgery.

Opening his eyes, the president told her, "Honey, I forgot to duck." Spying his lawyer, Edwin Meese III, Reagan asked, "Who's minding the store?"

That was a good question. Conditions at the White House were almost as chaotic as at the scene of the attempted assassination. At the time of the shooting, Vice President George H. W. Bush was in Austin, Texas, preparing to talk to state legislators. He immediately reboarded his plane to head back to Washington.

With the commander in chief under anesthesia and the second-in-command in the air, cabinet members gathered in the Situation Room at the White House. This is the secure military command area in the basement that maintains communications lines to the Pentagon, embassies, and official aircraft. There, two agency heads jockeyed to take charge of the country.

Secretary of State Alexander Haig announced, "I am in control here in the White House." This was an unexpected statement. Only days earlier the president had named Bush, not Haig, the head of crisis management. At the same time, Secretary of Defense Caspar Weinberger asserted that he had the right to take over. The jostling arose not only from strong personalities eager to increase their power but also from confusion or disagreement about the line of succession.

When the president and then the vice president are incapacitated, the Secretary of State becomes commander in chief. This system, called the normal command structure, takes effect by a majority vote of the cabinet.

Another system, called the National Command Authority, occurs when the military is involved. In this case, the Secretary of Defense takes charge. Since the cabinet had assembled in the Situation Room, which is considered a military post, Weinberger presumed that he outranked Haig.

The cabinet considered both options and rejected them. One person said, "the men gathered in the Situation Room [did not] know what action they were authorized to take." If a major decision needed to be made, it wasn't clear who had ultimate authority. The country was, in effect, presidentless.

Meanwhile, Back in 1787 (and 1967)…

The Framers thoroughly exhausted themselves and each other figuring out how to select the president and what he should do once in office. With little further ado, they created the position of vice president to be sure that a president-in-waiting would be available in case the original one died or became disabled.

৯৯ ৵৵

The vice presidency is "the most insignificant office that ever the invention of man contrived…"

—Vice President John Adams

৯৯ ৵৵

They also gave Congress the right to pass a law ranking a succession of other officeholders who would move into the White House if something happens to the vice-president-turned-president—and on down the line.

৯৯ ৵৵

"In Case of the Removal of the President from Office, or of his Death, Resignation, or Inability to discharge the Powers and Duties of the said Office, the Same shall devolve on the Vice President, and the Congress may by Law provide for the Case of Removal, Death, Resignation or Inability, both of the President and Vice President, declaring what Officer shall then act as President, and such Officer shall act accordingly, until the

Disability be removed, or a President shall be elected."

—Article II, Section 1

໑ ໑

Congress has passed a series of such laws, most recently the Presidential Succession Act of 1947, which lists the order of succession for seventeen possible presidents after the vice president.

The Twenty-fifth Amendment, adopted in 1967, lays out in more detail who takes office under various instances of bad timing and unfortunate mishaps. It allows the vice president, along with a majority of cabinet officers, to declare a president "unable to discharge the powers and duties of his office" and then to take over until the president recovers.

This amendment became urgent after the assassination of President John F. Kennedy in 1963. Legislators realized that if the bullet to his head had entered and exited along a slightly different trajectory, Kennedy might have lived but in a severely impaired state, which would have been not only a personal but also a political disaster.

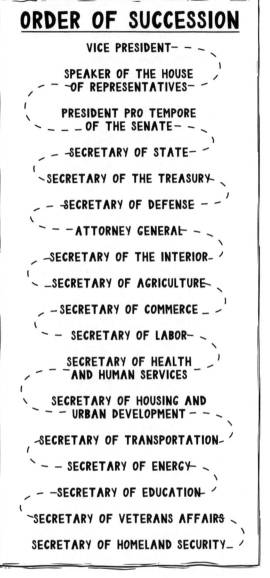

ORDER OF SUCCESSION

VICE PRESIDENT

SPEAKER OF THE HOUSE OF REPRESENTATIVES

PRESIDENT PRO TEMPORE OF THE SENATE

SECRETARY OF STATE

SECRETARY OF THE TREASURY

SECRETARY OF DEFENSE

ATTORNEY GENERAL

SECRETARY OF THE INTERIOR

SECRETARY OF AGRICULTURE

SECRETARY OF COMMERCE

SECRETARY OF LABOR

SECRETARY OF HEALTH AND HUMAN SERVICES

SECRETARY OF HOUSING AND URBAN DEVELOPMENT

SECRETARY OF TRANSPORTATION

SECRETARY OF ENERGY

SECRETARY OF EDUCATION

SECRETARY OF VETERANS AFFAIRS

SECRETARY OF HOMELAND SECURITY

The amendment also allows the president to replace the vice president, if that office becomes empty, with approval from Congress. This has happened twice. In 1973, President

Richard M. Nixon named Representative Gerald Ford to replace Vice President Spiro Agnew, who resigned after being charged with tax evasion. Then, when Nixon resigned, Ford became president and nominated New York's Governor Nelson Rockefeller to be his vice president.

Before signing off on their Constitution in 1787, the Framers added one more provision. To keep the executive and legislative branches separate, they clarified that people could hold only one government position at a time. Legislators could not simultaneously serve in the executive branch. It made sense at the time but could throw a wrench into the works in a present-day crisis.

೨೦ ೨೪

"...no Person holding any Office under the United States, shall be a Member of either House during his Continuance in Office."

—Article I, Section 6

೨೦ ೨೪

EAGLE HORIZON

Preparing for a possible nuclear war, President Jimmy Carter announced, "my intention is to stay here at the White House as long as I live to administer the affairs of government." He planned to send Vice President Walter Mondale to a secure location.

On 9/11, while Vice President Dick Cheney hunkered down in the White House, President George W. Bush flew around on Air Force One—whose communications systems were inadequate. A reporter wrote that Bush was "less informed than a normal civilian sitting at home watching the cable news."

These days, Eagle Horizon exercises carry out scenarios for nuclear accidents, chemical and cyberattacks, earthquakes, hurricanes, and other forms of mass destruction. These involve evacuating the president and other leadership as well as testing the preparedness of emergency teams.

So What's the Big Problem?

No constitution can cover every possible untoward event. Supreme Court Chief Justice John Marshall called the Constitution an outline rather than a detailed legal code. But sometimes outlines need to be filled in, and they're not always filled in properly.

Some people claim the Presidential Succession Act is an accident waiting to happen. The Speaker of the House is second in line, following the vice president. This person might belong to a different political party than the downed president and vice president. In the most recent election, the public might have opted for one party but the other one would now be in charge. Furthermore, most people interpret the Constitution to require the speaker to resign in order to take over the presidency, which means that the House would be left leaderless at a crucial time.

The Twenty-fifth Amendment was viewed as necessary to fill in parts of the outline sketched out in the Constitution. But it could potentially cause mischief. The key phrase "unable to discharge the powers and duties of his office" isn't defined. The president might be suffering from a physical ailment or dementia or a psychological problem, such as

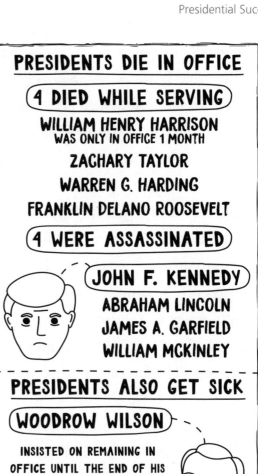

PRESIDENTS DIE IN OFFICE

4 DIED WHILE SERVING

WILLIAM HENRY HARRISON
WAS ONLY IN OFFICE 1 MONTH

ZACHARY TAYLOR

WARREN G. HARDING

FRANKLIN DELANO ROOSEVELT

4 WERE ASSASSINATED

JOHN F. KENNEDY

ABRAHAM LINCOLN

JAMES A. GARFIELD

WILLIAM MCKINLEY

PRESIDENTS ALSO GET SICK

WOODROW WILSON

INSISTED ON REMAINING IN OFFICE UNTIL THE END OF HIS TERM IN 1921, EVEN AFTER SUFFERING A SERIOUS STROKE IN 1919 THAT LEFT HIM PHYSICALLY AND MENTALLY DEBILITATED

DWIGHT D. EISENHOWER

SUFFERED BOTH A HEART ATTACK AND A STROKE WHILE PRESIDENT

HE BUCKED HIS DOCTOR'S ADVICE NOT TO RUN FOR RE ELECTION IN 1956 AND WON

FORTUNATELY, HIS HEALTH DID NOT DETERIORATE

depression or paranoia. A tug-of-war could arise if the vice president and cabinet secretaries squared off against a president they viewed as unfit to serve.

The country would face a constitutional crisis if a president resisted being described as unfit. Under those circumstances, Congress would have twenty-one days to choose between the president's claim that they're able to function versus that of the vice president and cabinet that the president is wrong. The president wins unless Congress, by a two-thirds vote in both houses, agrees with the vice president and cabinet that the president is unfit. Imagine the turmoil if only a majority of the members in one house agreed while two-thirds of the other house wanted to boot the president.

There Are Other Ways
States
Many states have detailed rules for succession in office, even for positions below the executive branch, though seven of them stop with the initial successor to the governor.

In forty-five states, the lieutenant governor becomes governor in case of a vacancy. In Maine and New Hampshire, the president of the state senate becomes governor. In Arizona, Oregon, and Wyoming, the successor is the secretary of state.

California explicitly states that the lieutenant governor can take over in the case of a "temporary disability" of the governor, though what counts as such a disability isn't defined.

The Montana constitution provides that the lieutenant governor becomes the "acting governor" if an illness or disability renders the governor incapable of performing the office, as well as whenever the governor has been absent from office for forty-five days.

Twenty states, including California and New York, require the governor to transfer power to the next official in line when leaving the state, even briefly. If a catastrophe occurs, the interim chief could end up being, say, a tax commissioner, who might be clueless

WHO'S GOT THE BALL?

A hypothetical scenario—which has become the basis for a television series—was prepared by the Brookings Institution and the American Enterprise Institute to demonstrate the utter chaos that would result from a disaster hitting right before the swearing-in ceremonies on Inauguration Day.

According to the scenario, terrorists detonate a small nuclear device on Pennsylvania Avenue between the White House and the Capitol. Everyone at those locations and in between is killed or immobilized. Without an incoming president, vice president, Speaker of the House, or president pro tempore, the presidency should pass to a member of the cabinet—but which one? (The president pro tempore is the most senior senator in the majority party and presides over the Senate when the vice president is absent.)

The president-elect hasn't taken office or confirmed a cabinet. An outgoing cabinet officer who hasn't resigned and wasn't at the White House could get the job. Possibly the Secretary of Veterans Affairs could step unsteadily into the presidency.

Or if no one in the constitutional line of succession is alive, a number of generals, undersecretaries, and governors might claim they are in charge. Undoubtedly, bitter arguments and political feuds would result. And Americans might not accept the person who gains power as a legitimate official.

about issues related to the governorship. In contrast, the president of the United States is always fully empowered, regardless of how far they are from home.

Other Countries

Many countries have a line of succession, but the circumstances are no more spelled out than they are in the United States, and the line is generally shorter.

The line of succession in the Statutes of the Republic of South Africa is only four levels deep and is triggered, vaguely, when the executive is "absent from the Republic or otherwise unable to fulfill the duties."

If the French presidency becomes vacant or if the cabinet declares that person incapacitated, the Constitution calls for election of a new president within twenty to thirty-five days. Meanwhile, the president of the Senate or, if that person is incapacitated, the cabinet, is in charge. Which cabinet member is a matter of debate.

The Brazilian Federal Constitution establishes that a vice president succeeds as president when the elected president dies, resigns, or is removed from office. The other officers in the line of succession are the presidents of the Chamber of Deputies, the Federal Senate, and the Supreme Federal Court, who serve in that order as Acting President. After President Dilma Rousseff was impeached in 2016, Vice President Michel Temer took over, but his political views were very different from hers. In 2017, he was accused of financial scandals but refused to resign despite widespread protests. He was finally replaced in 2019, following an election the previous year.

The vice president of India takes over for an absent or ill president, though the constitution does not spell out the circumstances. If that person is unavailable, a series of judges takes over until a new president is elected.

Presidential succession poses dilemmas around the world.

The United States

Since Reagan's shooting, every president has filed a plan for when and how the Twenty-fifth Amendment would come into play. However, these plans have remained classified. There is no way to know whether subsequent presidents have agreed on the details enough to clarify the ambiguities in the amendment.

Congress could pass a law that clarifies the situation, but it has not done so.

The Story Continues

If the gap in leadership after the shooting of President Reagan had lasted longer, there could have been a brawl involving the vice president, the cabinet, Congress, the Supreme Court, and hordes of lawyers. Fortunately, Bush landed in DC within hours, and Reagan returned to the Oval Office two weeks later.

CHAPTER 17

The Duck's In Charge. January 20.
Inauguration Day

"America Will Answer the Call"
During the spring and summer of 1992, television news programs aired wrenching images of emaciated children in Somalia. Civil war and anarchy in the East African country had caused widespread famine, and hundreds of thousands of Somalis, many of them infants and toddlers, were starving to death. The United Nations tried to deliver food, but armed gangs hijacked the cargo and assaulted aid workers. Conditions were deteriorating miserably.

In the fall, Boutros Boutros-Ghali, the secretary-general of the UN, appealed to its member nations, including the United States, to send military forces to Somalia. The troops wouldn't fight, he assured them; they would just stop the looting so food could be distributed.

On December 4, 1992, President George H. W. Bush addressed the American public about the tragedies and outrages in Somalia. This date fell four weeks after the presidential election, which he had lost to Bill Clinton. Bush had received only 40 percent of the vote and would be out of office in six weeks on January 20, 1993.

Bush ordered 25,000 marines, air force personnel, and soldiers to Somalia. He did not consult with Clinton or ask Congress for approval. After all, he was still commander in chief.

❧ ❧

"I have today told Secretary-General Boutros-Ghali that America will answer the call... As I speak, a Marine Amphibious ready group...is offshore Mogadishu [the capital]...
These and other American forces will assist in Operation Restore Hope."

—President George H. W. Bush

❧ ❧

This action was controversial. The president assured the country that the soldiers' mission was humanitarian, not military. He even promised that they'd be home by Inauguration Day, when Clinton would take over. Yet, he acknowledged, "we will not tolerate armed gangs." To many people, Bush sounded contradictory, and Operation Restore Hope sounded doomed.

President Clinton moved into the Oval Office as scheduled—but the troops hadn't moved back home. Clinton believed he had no choice but to continue Bush's policy.

As the months staggered on, armed Somalis attacked American soldiers, making food distribution nearly impossible. By the fall, the mission had changed from humanitarian aid to restoring a working government in Somalia—a goal no one in the Clinton administration had signed on for.

In October 1993, a foray that was supposed to be a quick arrest of two enemy leaders turned into a bloody fifteen-hour military battle. Rebels captured an American pilot, brutally murdered eighteen soldiers, and wounded another eighty-four. Hundreds, possibly thousands, of Somalis were killed. These horrifying events were depicted in the movie *Black Hawk Down*.

Clinton faced a dilemma. If he withdrew American forces from Somalia, his critics would charge that he was weak and unwilling to use the military to stand firm against threats to our country or to protect oppressed people. If he sent more troops to attack the rebels, they wouldn't be able to distribute food, and more Americans would surely die. This quandary was not one of

Clinton's making; he had inherited a complicated and messy situation created by an outgoing administration rejected by the electorate.

Meanwhile, Back in 1787 (and 1933)...

After considerable debate and uncertainty, the Framers established the president's term as four years.

༉ ༀ

"The executive Power shall be vested in a President of the United States of America. He shall hold his Office during the Term of four Years..."

—Article II, Section 1

༉ ༀ

But the Framers did not specify exactly when the term would begin or end. George Washington was first inaugurated on April 30, 1789; his second inauguration occurred on March 4, 1793. Why wasn't the second one also on April 30?

The first United States Congress to meet under the new Constitution was to convene on March 4, 1789, although a quorum didn't gather until April 5. Yet, March 4 was established as the starting point for measuring all terms of office, including the presidency and members of the House and Senate. And it lasted for 139 years.

In 1932, the world was in the midst of the Great Depression. Herbert Hoover was a terribly unpopular president running for a second term. If a new president was to replace Hoover, that person would have to wait until March 4, 1933, to get to work. The country did not want useless or harmful outgoing presidents to hang around. So, on March 2, 1932, Congress proposed the Twentieth Amendment, which moved Inauguration Day to January 20, beginning in 1937. A minimum of thirty-six states were needed to ratify the amendment—and it took only thirteen months for them to do so.

Like Washington, Franklin Delano Roosevelt, who succeeded Hoover, had a short first term. He was inaugurated under the old rules on March 4, 1933, but his second term began on January 20, 1937.

So What's the Big Problem?

The Twentieth Amendment reduced the period between the election and inauguration from four months to less than three months. But that still leaves a lot of time for departing presidents, often called "lame ducks," to cause trouble for their successors. They might do so by doing nothing during a crisis, like Hoover. Or they might make one worse by doing too much, like Bush. A president on their way out the door might make a monumental decision that should be made by the one who was recently elected—the person who would have to implement it.

If Inauguration Day took place shortly after the election, Clinton would have been able to make his own decisions about Somalia, and Roosevelt could have started pulling America out of the depression. But the Constitution prevents the people's choice from taking speedy action.

The reason is linked to the Electoral College. If a majority of that group can't agree on a winner, then the House of Representatives picks the president from the top three electoral vote-getters, and the Senate names the vice president. But since some representatives undoubtedly lost their seats in the election, it's the incoming congresspeople who are assigned the job. And they aren't sworn in until the first Monday in January.

"WAIT! I'M NOT READY."

Presidential candidates generally line up top White House aides and cabinet members even before the election. They use the time between then and their inauguration to fill in remaining posts and to solicit support from senators for the positions that need to be confirmed.

Reporters speculated that Donald J. Trump did not expect to win the election and had not picked his staff in preparation for stepping into the Oval Office. Well into his second year, hundreds of positions, including ambassadors and judges, remained unfilled.

There Are Other Ways

States

All states inaugurate governors more quickly than the national government does presidents. For example, Alaska and Hawaii hold inaugurations in early December, less than a month after Election Day. New York inaugurates on New Year's Day.

WHERE DID LAME DUCKS COME FROM?

Around the time the Framers were writing the Constitution, English people called businessmen who couldn't pay off their debts "lame ducks" because they waddled away. In the early twentieth century, an American magazine referred to losing candidates that way because their wings had been clipped.

Other Countries

No other country relies on an electoral college, which requires time to convene, so no other country waits months between selecting a new leader and letting that person lead. The president of France generally takes office within ten days of the election. In Great Britain, a newly elected prime minister takes office the day after the election.

The United States

If Inauguration Day occurred shortly after Election Day, the American people would be led by the person they've elected to office rather than by a lame duck. Because the inauguration date is inscribed in the Constitution, changing it would require an amendment.

Until the Electoral College is eliminated, which would also require amending the Constitution, Inauguration Day has to be postponed in case the result on Election Day is not decisive.

The Story Continues

Following the Black Hawk Down tragedy in October 1993, Clinton sent more Marines and armored tanks to Somalia, not to fight but to support the withdrawal of the soldiers already there. They negotiated the release of the captured pilot, and almost all American troops left the country by the end of March 1994.

Operation Restore Hope saved thousands of Somalis from starvation but did not establish a working government. The events remained a black mark on Clinton's presidency.

NEXT!

Probably the most dramatic example of one leader immediately replacing another was the defeat of Prime Minister Winston Churchill in the British election of July 1945. He had heroically led World War II efforts, but a majority of Brits was not confident he would be a great peacetime leader. They replaced him with Clement Attlee of the opposition Labour Party two months after Germany surrendered in Europe but before the war ended in Asia.

Churchill was in Potsdam, Germany, at a conference that included US President Harry S. Truman and Prime Minister Josef Stalin of the Soviet Union. They were discussing the shape of the postwar world, including how to end the war against Japan. Attlee flew to Potsdam and took over the chair in which Churchill had been sitting. Churchill returned to London.

PART VII
Emergency! Emergency!

In this section, we continue to deal with the ways the Constitution can trip us up at the worst possible time—when we are involved in wars of various sorts. In these situations, the victims of the Constitution's fault lines aren't members of Congress or the president. They're ordinary citizens—possibly you.

We consider

- limitations on what you can say during wartime and
- ways the government can restrict your freedom of movement during an epidemic.

CHAPTER 18

At War
Emergency Powers

"Disloyal, Profane, Scurrilous, or Abusive Language"

By February 1917, World War I had been raging in Europe and the Middle East for two and a half years, but most Americans had no interest in entering the war. The issues those regions were fighting about—mostly ethnic and economic tensions—seemed confined to Europe and irrelevant to the United States. Besides that, battlefield conditions, Americans had heard, were dreadful. In just four months over the summer and fall of 1916, a million soldiers had died at the Battle of the Somme. It wasn't surprising that President Woodrow Wilson was reelected with the slogan "He kept us out of war."

But then a telegram surfaced in which the German foreign minister threatened to torpedo American ships. Outraged, Wilson changed his mind and asked Congress to declare war on the Central Powers.

୬ ୬

"The world must be made safe for democracy."

—President Woodrow Wilson

୬ ୬

Congress agreed. Members adopted a resolution to go to war and passed several related laws.

• The Selective Service Act required men in their twenties to register for the draft.

• The Espionage Act of 1917 made it criminal to obstruct the draft and to send unpatriotic materials through the mail.

• The Sedition Act of 1918 declared it a federal offense to use "disloyal, profane, scurrilous, or abusive language" about the Constitution or the American government, flag, or military uniform.

Most Americans quickly caught war fever.

• Three million soldiers were inducted.

• Millions of other people volunteered to work on the home front.

• Restaurants replaced sauerkraut with "Liberty Cabbage."

• Nebraska even banned teaching German.

Patriotism wasn't merely important; it was a political and social imperative.

But despite the fervor and the new laws, some people continued to oppose America's involvement in the Great War. One was a man named Eugene V. Debs.

When he was fourteen, Debs dropped out of school to work on the railroads. Seeing how railroad owners amassed fortunes while the laborers remained impoverished, he demanded higher pay and organized strikes against management.

Over time, he joined and then led the Socialist Party of America. Socialists argued that there should be no private ownership of businesses or property. Everything should be shared. In the 1912 election, Debs ran for president under its banner, and more than nine hundred thousand people voted for him.

Debs believed that wars are similar to railroads. They are undertaken to benefit the wealthy—but are built and operated by the downtrodden. In June 1918, days after nearly ten thousand American soldiers were slaughtered at a battle site in France, Debs spoke to supporters at an outdoor rally in Canton, Ohio.

Rulers, Debs declared, "have always taught and trained you to believe it to be your patriotic duty to go to war and to have yourselves slaughtered at their command. But in all the history of the world you, the people, have never had a voice in declaring war."

Debs understood that the government might consider his speech disloyal. Nevertheless, he concluded, "Do not worry about the charge of treason."

❧ ❧

"…it is extremely dangerous to exercise the constitutional right of free speech in a country fighting to make democracy safe for the world."

—Eugene V. Debs

❧ ❧

He had not directly urged the crowd to rebel or to resist conscription. However, he praised three people who were in jail for obstructing the draft. In addition, the Socialist Party had recently adopted a resolution calling for "continuous, active, and public opposition to the war, through demonstrations, mass petitions, and all other means within our power."

Federal agents, who had been shadowing Debs, wrote down his words. Debs was arrested, tried, and convicted of violating the Espionage Act of 1917. He was sentenced to ten years in prison.

Debs's lawyers appealed to the Supreme Court, arguing that he had a right to free speech and that, in any case, he hadn't advised anyone to desert or resist conscription.

Writing for a unanimous court, Justice Oliver Wendell Holmes Jr. disagreed. Even though Debs did not explicitly tell his listeners to avoid the draft, that idea was the gist of his talk. And his words, according to Holmes, "create[d] a clear and present danger" to a country at war. He concluded that "no Court could regard them as protected by a constitutional right."

❧ ❧

"When a nation is at war many things that might be said in time of peace are such a hindrance to its effort that their utterances will not be endured so long as men fight."

—Supreme Court Oliver Wendell Holmes Jr.

❧ ❧

Debs, according to the court, was endangering the country during a time of emergency. And so he must remain imprisoned.

Meanwhile, Back in ~~1787~~ 1791...

When the Framers gathered in Philadelphia to write a new constitution, they were already breaking the rules. Congress's authorization specified that only limited revisions to the Articles of Confederation could be made. But the Framers believed that the fate of the country was at stake—definitely an emergency that warranted wholesale changes to form a new kind of government.

୨ ଏ

"...in certain seasons of public danger it is commendable to exceed power."

—George Mason, Virginia

୨ ଏ

By mid-September 1787, they were ready to put the finishing touches on their handiwork and cart it off to the states for ratification. A few issues remained, however. One of these was a Bill of Rights.

Many state constitutions guaranteed their citizens fundamental rights, such as freedom of religion and of speech. The Framers discussed including such a Bill of Rights in the Constitution but James Madison of Virginia argued that lists of this, that, and the other rights were no better than "parchment barriers"—not worth the paper they were written on. The government could shred, burn, or ink them out the moment it felt threatened. After a few minutes of debate, the Framers voted unanimously not to include it.

Their reasoning was that they were creating a government with limited powers. Alexander Hamilton of New York pointed out that if a particular power, such as restricting freedom of speech, was not specifically granted to the government, then officials didn't have it. So why bother to tell people they could speak freely if those in power couldn't tell them not to?

During the ratification process, however, the public clamored for guaranteed rights, and supporters agreed to add them as the first order of business in the new government.

Madison was convinced, and, after he was elected a representative from Virginia in the First United States Congress, he became the chief draftsman of the Bill of Rights. (Twelve amendments were submitted to the states for ratification but only Amendments Three through Twelve were ratified by 1791.)

What we call the First Amendment (originally the Third) opens powerfully and without compromise.

        ❧ ❧

"Congress shall make no law... abridging the freedom of speech..."

—First Amendment

        ❧ ❧

If there can really be "no law" that limits what people can say, how could Congress pass the Sedition Act of 1918, which made it a crime to use abusive language about the government?

The Constitution wouldn't have been written if the Framers hadn't disobeyed rules and exceeded powers specified in the Articles of Confederation. A dozen years earlier, the country was founded on a revolution. Maybe it's not surprising, then, that future members of Congress believed that in some cases they, too, could disobey the Constitution's rules. This was especially the case when they faced emergencies.

In 1798, just seven years after the Bill of Rights was adopted, Congress passed a Sedition Act while America was involved in what was called a "quasi-war" of naval incidents against France. Several dozen newspaper writers who criticized the government were arrested, including one who had merely expressed his wish that a cannonball would wallop President John Adams in the rear.

When the journalists complained that they were being deprived of their rights under the First Amendment, government leaders responded that the Constitution allows Congress to bar sedition. After all, promoting disrespect of the president, especially during a crisis, threatened the "domestic tranquility" promised in the Preamble. The reporters were jailed.

Thomas Jefferson, the next president, believed the act was unconstitutional and in 1801 pardoned those who remained in prison.

So What's the Big Problem?

Debs's case raises questions about whether or not we lose our rights when the president and Congress agree that our country is threatened. The Constitution barely addresses what are called "emergency powers"—the additional authority that the government might assume during a war or other crisis. It seemed to Debs and many other people that his oration was protected by his First Amendment right to free speech. But the US government disagreed.

By supporting opponents of the war and urging his listeners not to become cannon fodder, was Debs encouraging people to disobey a law, resist the draft, and rebel against the government? Or

WILL THIS EMERGENCY EVER END?

During an emergency in ancient Rome, a constitutional dictator could be appointed and handed nearly absolute power, but only for up to six months. The situation is different in modern America. Presidents can declare an emergency and use laws passed by Congress to take charge of many aspects of military and civilian life.

However, emergencies here are hardly ever officially called off. In 1976, with several obsolete "emergencies" still on the books, Congress passed a law requiring presidents to request a renewal every year. Critics charge that the law has not just failed—it has given presidents an emergency blank check. As of early 2019, thirty-one states of emergency were in effect, the oldest one dating back to 1979.

was he merely using an inflammatory term—"cannon fodder"—to describe how soldiers were treated, without implying what his audience should then do? Does freedom of speech cover advocating breaking the law?

The same concerns about national security arose when America entered World War II in 1941. Two months after Japanese aircraft bombed Pearl Harbor, a US military base in Hawaii, President Franklin Delano Roosevelt banned all Americans who had Japanese ancestors from living in a large swath of the western United States. Because they were Asian, US law at the time already prevented them from ever becoming citizens, but their children, who were born in the United States, did hold citizenship. Roosevelt feared that some would be more loyal to the country of their forefathers than to the country in which they lived and, in many cases, in which they were citizens. The military rounded up more than 110,000 people of Japanese ancestry and confined them in internment camps, which were so miserable that Justice Owen Roberts called them concentration camps.

One Japanese-American man, Fred Korematsu, refused to follow orders and was jailed. He appealed to the Supreme Court but a majority of justices ruled against him in *Korematzu v. United States*. In this case, the court agreed with the president that during wartime it is more important to prevent possible threats to national security than to allow individuals their right to freedom. Although the court didn't say so, it came close to applying a maxim from ancient Rome: "In times of war, the laws fall silent."

The Framers defined danger as being under attack. Today we understand that peril can take many forms—not just cannons, but also technological, medical, biological, and environmental threats. How much does the Constitution control the decisions the government can make when we face a crisis? Does it speak clearly in defense of indi-

> ## FRED KOREMATSU—
> ## THE AFTERMATH
>
> In 1988, Congress passed a Civil Liberties Act, which President Ronald Reagan signed into law. The act formally apologized for the displacement and detention of Japanese-Americans and gave $20,000 to every person who had been displaced. President Bill Clinton bestowed the Presidential Medal of Freedom on Korematsu in 1998. And in 2011, California established January 30 as the annual Fred Korematsu Day of Civil Liberties and the Constitution.
>
> Seven years later, the Supreme Court abruptly overruled its original decision in the case. At the same time, though, the Court gave the president extensive power over immigration.

viduals? Or does it allow public officials to do whatever they think best? Was Madison right—is the Bill of Rights merely a parchment barrier?

There Are Other Ways
States

States often declare a state of emergency after a natural disaster like a hurricane, or during significant civic unrest, such as rioting. The situation might involve temporarily suspending citizens' ordinary rights by, for instance, imposing a curfew. But by the mid-twentieth century, courts agreed that there is no such thing as sedition or treason against a state as there is against a country.

Other Countries

War is the fundamental stress test for any democratic constitution because during such a crisis, leaders are tempted to take control and shut the people out of the process. Citizens clamor to be protected from enemies, yet they also want their freedoms protected.

Around the world, 178 countries have constitutions with emergency powers, which give the head of state the ability to suspend all or some of the people's rights. Forty-six European countries, including Russia, have signed onto the European Convention on Human Rights.

Article 10 of this document is far more detailed than the First Amendment to our Constitution.

ॐ ॐ

1. Everyone has the right to freedom of expression. This right shall include freedom to hold opinions and to receive and impart information and ideas without interference by public authority…

2. The exercise of these freedoms, since it carries with it duties and responsibilities, may be subject to such…restrictions or penalties as are prescribed by law and are necessary in a democratic society, in the interests of national security, territorial integrity or public safety, for the prevention of disorder or crime, for the protection of health or morals, for the protection of the reputation or the rights of others, for preventing the disclosure

of information received in confidence, or for maintaining the authority and impartiality of the judiciary.

—Article 10, European Convention on Human Rights

ॐ ॐ

The United States
Perhaps the Constitution should be amended to define more clearly when the country faces a true emergency and what the government can and cannot do.

The Story Continues

Holmes later admitted that he had found the issue a tough one to decide. "I hated to have to write the Debs case," he wrote to a friend. "I could not see the wisdom of pressing the cases, especially when the fighting was over."

The Great War ended on November 11, 1918. The decision in *Debs v. United States* was handed down in 1919. The justice probably knew that Debs was no longer endangering America. Nevertheless, he didn't change his mind, though he added, "I think it quite possible that if I had been on the jury I should have been for acquittal."

Debs appealed to Wilson to pardon him, but the president refused. "This man was a traitor to his country," Wilson declared, "and he will never be pardoned during my administration."

In 1920, Debs ran for the presidency for the fifth time. During this campaign he was imprisoned, so he was identified on ballots as Prisoner 9653. Again, over nine hundred thousand people voted for

him. The winner of the election, Warren G. Harding, a Republican, commuted Debs's sentence on Christmas Day in 1921 and invited him to the White House.

"I have heard so damned much about you, Mr. Debs, that now I am very glad to meet you personally."

—President Warren G. Harding

CHAPTER 19

At War with Bugs
Habeas Corpus

A "National Security Priority"

In March 2014, officials finally identified the disease that, in the previous three months, had killed fifty-nine residents of the West African country of Guinea. Ebola virus disease, a zoonosis (an illness that can leap from animals to humans) had already crossed borders, infecting people in Sierra Leone and Liberia. From there, Ebola went, well, viral. The disease spread rapidly; many people were concerned that it would also go global.

In December 2013, the first victim, a one-year-old child in Guinea, died days after he spiked a fever, vomited, and spewed black feces. Within weeks, his sister and mother, and three women who cleaned their house suffered the same symptoms and also died. When his grandmother got sick, she sought treatment in another town. She died, as did her doctor and the people who buried her and her doctor.

In October 2014, two nurses in Texas who had cared for an American with Ebola became infected.

President Barack Obama declared Ebola a "national security priority." Some members of Congress called for a travel ban between the United States and West Africa.

On October 24, 2014, the governors of New York, New Jersey, and Illinois—two Democrats and one Republican—issued a mandate: all

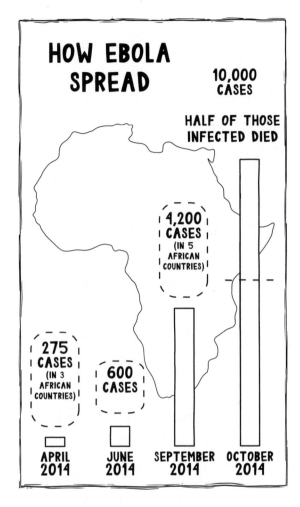

HOW EBOLA SPREAD

10,000 CASES

HALF OF THOSE INFECTED DIED

4,200 CASES (IN 5 AFRICAN COUNTRIES)

275 CASES (IN 3 AFRICAN COUNTRIES)

600 CASES

APRIL 2014

JUNE 2014

SEPTEMBER 2014

OCTOBER 2014

health-care workers who had contact with Ebola patients in West Africa must be quarantined for twenty-one days upon entering the United States.

At 1:00 that afternoon, Kaci Hickox landed in Newark, New Jersey. A specialist in tropical nursing who had worked for ten years in medical hotspots around the world, she had spent the previous six weeks caring for Ebola patients in Sierra Leone. The night before she left, she'd treated a ten-year-old girl for seizures; to her dismay, the child died. Hickox's trip home took two days, and she arrived exhausted and hungry.

When she told an airport immigration officer where she had been, he donned a mask and gloves, then took her to a quarantine office. A series of people dressed in coveralls, gloves, and face shields—and one wearing a weapons belt—questioned her.

Two people took her temperature but one did so inaccurately and jumped to the conclusion that she had a fever, which can be the first sign of Ebola infection. Hickox was zipped into a hazmat suit and put into an ambulance. Eight police cars, lights flashing and sirens blaring, escorted her from the airport to a tent in a hospital parking lot, where she was ordered to stay.

A doctor took her temperature: normal. A technician tested her blood for Ebola: negative.

Dr. Thomas Frieden, the director of the Centers for Disease Control and Prevention (CDC), a federal agency, clarified that it was not necessary to quarantine Hickox. No fever: no danger. She simply needed to check her temperature twice a day for twenty-one days.

Obama protested her detention. Nevertheless, New Jersey Governor Chris Christie demanded that Hickox remain isolated in the unheated tent, wearing only paper scrubs.

After two days, Hickox hired a civil rights lawyer to argue her case against the state of New Jersey. "I feel like my basic human rights have been violated," Hickox said, calling the state's actions not "Constitutionally just."

The next day, after Hickox again tested negative, Christie released her— on the condition that she proceed directly to her home in northern Maine. That state's governor, Paul LePage, insisted that she remain there for three days and then follow the CDC's guidelines.

On her journey from New Jersey to Maine, Hickox passed through five other states, including New York, whose governor had imposed the same quarantine restrictions as New Jersey. If he had apprehended her en route, she would have had to threaten to take him to court, too, to release her.

"I remain appalled by these home quarantine policies that have been forced upon me, even though I am in perfectly good health," Hickox stated. "I will go to court to fight for my freedom."

❧ ❧

"The conditions that the state of Maine is now requiring Kaci to comply with are unconstitutional and illegal and there is no justification for the state of Maine to infringe on her liberty."

—Norman Siegel, *Kaci Hickox's lawyer*

❧ ❧

In response, LePage took Hickox to court to enforce the quarantine. He also posted state police outside her home.

Meanwhile, Back in 1787...

One of the rights, in addition to freedom of speech, that the Framers considered including in the Constitution was the writ of habeas corpus. This is a court order with a Latin term meaning "that you have the body." It guarantees a person who has been imprisoned the right to produce what is called the great writ, which directs the court to either release the prisoner or explain why the government has the power to keep the person in jail.

The colonists were accustomed to the right of habeas corpus because the British had guaranteed this protection to citizens for more than a century. Some people traced it back to Magna Carta in 1215. Nevertheless, through most of the summer, the Framers did not include it in the Constitution. They considered it one of those basic rights that belonged in a Bill of Rights.

In August, they returned to the issue. Alexander Hamilton of New York argued that habeas corpus belonged in the Constitution proper. He quoted William Blackstone, a British judge, who had said "confinement of the person, by secretly hurrying him to jail, where his sufferings are unknown or forgotten" was the worst form of tyranny. Hamilton labeled unjustified imprisonment a "fatal evil."

Other Framers agreed with Hamilton, although they debated whether to include exceptions—circumstances under which protection against long-term imprisonment could be halted. Gouverneur Morris of Pennsylvania proposed that "Rebellion or invasion" would justify suspending the right of habeas corpus. Nearing the end of their work, the Framers agreed to incorporate habeas corpus, with Morris's exception, into the Constitution.

❧ ❧

"The Privilege of the Writ of Habeas Corpus shall not be suspended, unless when in Cases of Rebellion or Invasion the public Safety may require it."

—Article I, Section 9

❧ ❧

The first Congress then passed a law giving US courts the power to issue writs—court orders—to enforce this provision. They could do so by demanding that the government justify detentions and, if it could not, then demanding release of the prisoner.

But how would this right be protected? The Framers addressed the system, called due process, in the Fifth Amendment, part of the Bill of Rights. It guaranteed individuals the right to protect their very lives, freedom, and goods through a legal process, such as by making their case in a court of law.

In 1833, the Supreme Court decided that the Fifth Amendment applied only to the national government, so the Fourteenth Amendment was added in 1868. It is identical to the Fifth Amendment, except that it applies to state governments.

But in times of rebellion or invasion, the government does not necessarily have to follow these rules. During these times the writ of habeas corpus can be suspended, and suspects can be kept in jail indefinitely without any official having to explain why.

In the past, presidents have claimed sweeping powers when they decide "the public Safety may require it." President Abraham Lincoln came to this conclusion shortly after the start of the Civil War.

John Merryman, a farmer and militiaman from Maryland, was accused of destroying railroad tracks, a bridge, and telegraph lines in order to prevent Union soldiers from defending Washington, DC, against rebel attacks. He was arrested and imprisoned for treason.

Lincoln suspended habeas corpus for everyone in the area. Merryman demanded the great writ. Lincoln ordered the jailer to reject all writs "most respectfully...[until] the present unhappy difficulties are at an end."

Many Americans from both North and South objected strongly to Lincoln's suspending the writ, arguing that only

Congress could take this drastic action. But the president responded, "the Constitution itself, is silent as to which, or who, is to exercise the power... I think the man whom, for the time, the people have, under the constitution, made the commander-in-chief, of their Army and Navy, is the man who holds the power."

Merryman's case went to a federal circuit court presided over by Supreme Court Chief Justice Roger B. Taney. The judge accused Lincoln of grabbing "a power which he does not possess under the Constitution." Taney pointed out that even the English monarch couldn't suspend habeas corpus without approval by Parliament. Consequently, the justice concluded, "the people of the United States are no longer living under a Government of laws." Instead, he asserted, they were living in a military dictatorship. While many people agreed with Taney, others praised Lincoln for doing what was necessary to defend the union and, therefore, constitutional order.

So What's the Big Problem?

In addition to military situations, nowadays we face many possible emergencies that didn't occur to the Framers. These include not only public health hazards but also cyberterrorism, telecommunications shutdowns, natural disasters, and economic crises. In these frightening instances, we might need someone who can make fast, unquestioned decisions. But it's not clear who has the authority to do what. And shouldn't a constitution specify or limit what that person can do?

Really, I'm Fine. Uh-oh.

The habeas corpus clause limits the federal government's ability to suspend habeas corpus to cases of "Rebellion or Invasion." Can an infectious microbe be considered an invasion, like a foreign army?

Compared to other possible epidemics, Ebola is easy to address. Because victims develop a fever before they become contagious, no one, including nurses who travel from affected countries, needs to be restrained until and unless they develop symptoms.

But other diseases, such as influenzas that have killed millions, can be spread by people who do not yet show signs of being sick. If there is an outbreak of such an epidemic, can—or should—the president order everyone in the country to stay at home, whether or not they seem sick, or confine them if they insist on leaving home?

That's an (Executive) Order!

Congress has authorized the president to issue an executive order identifying particular diseases as "quarantinable." With that, US law allows the president to order the "apprehension, detention, or conditional release of individuals… for the purpose of preventing the introduction, transmission, or spread of such communicable diseases…" If the president issues this executive order, the CDC's powers to oversee these processes kick in.

Article I, Section 8 of the Constitution, known as the Commerce Clause, gives Congress the "power…to regulate commerce with foreign nations, and among the several states, and with the Indian tribes." In the late eighteenth century this had nothing to do with emergencies. But today, the CDC uses this clause to justify Congress's ability to delegate authority for imposing isolation and quarantine in some situations. Traffic in sick people, the CDC asserts, is the same as traffic in cars or washing machines or any other product that crosses borders.

The Long Arm of the State

The authority to enforce quarantine and isolation are among the "police powers"—the protection of the public health, safety, and welfare—that states commonly carry out. States can't violate the US Constitution, but they are given wide latitude in defining such protection. States have often expanded their authority in cases of public health emergencies.

In 2001, several congressmen received envelopes in the mail that contained anthrax, a poisonous powder. In response to this biohazard threat, the CDC asked lawyers and health specialists to draft a set of laws that state legislatures could adopt before another threat loomed. They came up with the Model State Emergency Health Powers Act. So far, around forty states have introduced their own versions of this act.

As a result, various states are allowed to do some or all of the following:

• Define "public health emergency" almost however they like.

• Require pharmacists to report prescriptions to the government.

• "Commandeer or utilize any private property...necessary to cope with the emergency." Property owners cannot claim a right to keep their land and will not necessarily be paid for their losses.

State governments might well need to take some of these actions so that health officials can curtail the spread of what they fear are epidemics. But both liberals and conservatives have strongly criticized these broad powers that states have given themselves.

• The liberal American Civil Liberties Union pointed out that officials could enforce quarantines with no justification—just as New Jersey and Maine did regarding Ebola.

• Phyllis Schlafly, a conservative lawyer, labeled such quarantines "an unprecedented assault on the constitutional rights of the American people."

• The Association of American Physicians and Surgeons warned that such "model" laws turn "governors into dictators."

Furthermore, with each state developing its own laws, the country could become a crazy quilt of rules and procedures. Hickox was subject to quarantine in three of the six states she passed through but could travel freely through three others. In a full-on emergency, how would travelers know which states they could traverse and where they could be apprehended?

There Are Other Ways

States

Although states might try, they cannot suspend due process and round people up in times of emergency. Most states do give their governors the power to call out the National Guard under many more circumstances than just rebellion or invasion. Florida's constitution, for instance, states, "The governor shall have power to call out the militia to preserve the public peace, execute the laws of the state, suppress insurrection, or repel invasion."

Governors tend to use this power in cases of severe weather, such as hurricanes, violent demonstrations, or mass shootings, as Florida's Governor Rick Scott did in 2016.

In 2018, the governors of Texas and Arizona deployed troops along the US–Mexico border in support of President Donald J. Trump's zero-tolerance immigration policies. There was disagreement about whether the arrival of several thousand people seeking jobs and safety in the United States amounted to an emergency, though Trump declared it to be one the following year and vetoed Congress's attempt to override it.

In other disease-related news, Jay Inslee, the governor of Washington, declared an emergency there because of a measles outbreak in 2019. Going a step further, a county executive in New York barred all children who had not been vaccinated against measles from appearing in public. Ten days later, a judge overruled the order. Then, the major of New York ordered everyone in four boroughs to be vaccinated. It's not clear who's in charge during medical emergencies.

Other Countries

The constitution of South Africa offers a modern model of emergency powers. Here are its main features:

- Only the national legislature—not the president or the courts—can declare a state of emergency.

- The Constitution recognizes many kinds of emergencies, including "war, invasion, general insurrection, disorder, natural disaster, or other public emergency."

- Parliament can declare a state of emergency only when two conditions are met: "(a) the life of the nation is threatened by [these circumstances] and; (b) the declaration is necessary to restore peace and order."

- A declared state of emergency can last no more than twenty-one days. It can be extended by the lower house of Parliament, but only for three months at a time. After the first extension, at least 60 percent of the lower house must agree to another one.

- Even then, the courts can determine whether or not the emergency is valid and, if so, whether any "action taken in consequence of a declaration" is valid. That is, the courts can overrule Parliament's declaration and any emergency laws it passes.

The South African Constitutional Court has not had an occasion to rule on a state of emergency. But the Constitutional Court of Colombia has twice ruled emergencies declared by the president to be illegal.

The United States

The Constitution would serve the country better if it were amended to spell out more clearly and in more detail the actions particular federal officials could take in times of crisis. In addition, the definition of crisis needs to include more than invasion and rebellion.

The Story Continues

Several days after LePage tried to confine Hickox to her home, the legal system in Maine ruled in her favor.

༄ ༄

"The court is fully aware of the misconceptions, misinformation, bad science, and bad information being spread from shore to shore in our country with respect to Ebola. The court is fully aware that people are acting out of fear and that this fear is not entirely rational."

—Judge Charles C. LaVerdiere

ﳞ ﳝ

Hickox responded by calling it "a good day" and added that her "thoughts, prayers, and gratitude" were with her patients in West Africa. The governor replied, "I don't trust her."

She also won her suit against New Jersey. Rather than take payment for her pain and suffering, she asked the court to tell the state that it must allow people who are quarantined to contest the order confining them.

In early 2017, the CDC adopted rules that allow the federal government to impose national quarantines and prohibit travel from one state to another. In 2018, the Trump administration disbanded the Global Health Security Team, which was in charge of our country's response in case of a pandemic.

Authorities are likely to get into a free-for-all at the first uncertain sign of such an emergency.

CHAPTER 20

We Can Change It, Right?
Amending the Constitution

"A Woman Should Have the Right"

"Equality of rights under the law shall not be abridged by the United States or by any State on account of sex."

Phyllis Schlafly—mother, lawyer, and political activist—had long felt not only incensed but also deeply concerned about this proposed Equal Rights Amendment (ERA). It was worrisome enough that the ERA had passed both houses of Congress within a year—first in the House of Representatives in 1971 and then in the Senate in 1972.

Worse, by 1979, thirty-five states had approved the ERA. Thirty had done so in the first year—Hawaii only minutes after Congress adopted it! With support from only three more states, she feared that radical feminists, both women and their male supporters, would add their amendment to the Constitution.

Giving women all the same rights as men was a dangerous proposition, Schlafly believed. If equality was forced on women, they'd have to march into battle just like men, share bathrooms with men, and allow their ex-husbands to get custody of their children and stop paying alimony. Government-funded childcare would encourage women to go to work and pay less attention to their families. Single-sex organizations such as fraternities and sororities, Boy and Girl Scouts, and private schools and colleges would have to merge. Both abortions and gay rights would be legalized.

❧ ❧

"A woman should have the right to be in the home as a wife and mother."

—Phyllis Schlafly

❧ ❧

Schlafly was no softy. She had worked her way through college testing ammunition by firing rifles and machine guns at targets.

Her political opponents, especially the National Organization for Women (NOW), argued that the ERA was necessary to combat sex discrimination in the workplace, where women typically earned less and were awarded fewer promotions than men. It would also support women who were victims of sexual assault. Above all, they claimed, it would give women the same equal protection under the laws of the land that were granted to formerly enslaved people by the Fourteenth Amendment in 1868. So NOW revived the ERA, which had first been introduced into Congress in 1923, but had subsequently fallen into oblivion.

Schlafly predicted that, as a result of the ERA, women would actually end up less protected by the men in their lives than they had been before. To counteract these perils, she went on the defensive. To hold the line on the ERA, she formed an organization in 1972, called STOP ERA. The first word stood for Stop Taking Our Privileges.

Schlafly had reason to believe that her tactics were working. Initially even a majority of men had approved of the

STOP ERA SUPPORTERS IN ILLINOIS BROUGHT LEGISLATORS HOMEMADE JAM WITH NOTES READING

PRESERVE US FROM A
CONGRESSIONAL JAM

VOTE AGAINST THE
ERA SHAM

amendment. But support in the states had slowed considerably, and five states had even rescinded their ratification.

Beginning in 1918, Congress had usually placed seven-year time limits on the ratification of constitutional amendments. The legislation proposing the ERA was filed in 1971 and quickly passed in 1972. Proponents had until March 22, 1979, to round up the thirty-eight states necessary to ratify it. The problem was that NOW was demanding that Congress extend the deadline by three years to give them time to persuade another three states to sign on.

Schlafly was incensed and concerned: her opponents were relentless and might succeed. But she also knew she had the easier job. It's harder to get an amendment adopted than it is to stop one in its tracks.

Meanwhile, Back in 1787...

The bickering that had characterized the Framers' summer debates did not simmer down as fall approached. The

---

11,000 AND COUNTING

More than eleven thousand amendments to the Constitution have been proposed. A few would

- prohibit anyone involved in a duel from holding a federal office;
- choose the president by lot;
- prevent bankers from serving in Congress; and
- expel members of Congress who miss more than 40 percent of roll call votes on bills.

---

gentlemen enjoyed a cool spell the first week of September, but temperatures rose again during their last week together. So did their prickliness.

In addition to coming to an agreement on presidential vetoes, they also had to deal with how the new constitution could be changed after the states ratified it—assuming they did. The delegates' views about this new government ranged from deeply satisfied to profoundly troubled.

෨ ෫

"This constitution may be found to have defects in it; amendments hence may become necessary."

—James Wilson, Pennsylvania

෨ ෫

One of the fatal flaws of the Articles of Confederation was that it was practically impossible to amend: every state legislature had to agree to any change. Any state, whatever its size or population, could blackball a revision by vetoing it. It was partly because of that predicament that the Framers had started all over with a new constitution in Philadelphia.

The first proposal for an amendment process relied on state legislatures to call for another convention. On the other hand, Alexander Hamilton of New York wanted the federal government to be in charge; he proposed giving only Congress the right to summon a convention.

James Madison of Virginia feared that conventioneers might get carried away and undo all of the hard work the Framers had done during the previous four months. After all, the Framers had completely overturned the Articles, and it could happen again. After some debate, the Framers managed to concoct a more or less happy medium. Proposals for amendments could come up in two ways:

• Congress could propose an amendment when two-thirds of both houses saw the need.

• Or two-thirds of the states could petition for a special convention.

But proposing amendments is only half the job. The other half is ratifying them.

Madison raised the ante with requirements for ratification, though not so high as requiring unanimity, as in the Articles. Amendments would officially be added to the Constitution (or clauses would be deleted from it) only after three-quarters of the states approved. This approval could come from either the states' legislatures or special state conventions, whichever Congress decided to require.

This compromise satisfied almost all the Framers. But a contentious issue remained. Worried that free states would quickly alter the Constitution to hinder slavery, John Rutledge of South Carolina added a provision: no amendment could allow Congress to ban the international slave trade before 1808. In addition, the Senate would always be composed of two senators per state unless every state in the union agreed to a change.

Madison viewed the decision for every state to have the same number of votes in the Senate as an "evil." But, as with protecting the slave trade for twenty years, he argued it was the price that had to be paid to get a constitution. Article V sealed the deal by making these concessions unamendable.

ঔ ঌ

"The Congress, whenever two thirds of both Houses shall deem it necessary, shall propose Amendments to this Constitution, or, on the Application of the Legislatures of two thirds of the several States, shall call a Convention for proposing Amendments, which, in either Case, shall be valid to all Intents and Purposes, as Part of this Constitution, when ratified by the Legislatures of three fourths of the several States, or by Conventions in three fourths thereof, as the one or the other Mode of Ratification may be proposed by the Congress; Provided that no Amendment which may be made prior to the Year One thousand eight hundred and eight shall in any Manner affect the first and fourth Clauses in the Ninth Section of the first Article; and that no State, without its Consent, shall be deprived of its equal Suffrage in the Senate."

—Article V

ঔ ঌ

So What's the Big Problem?

It's very difficult to amend the Constitution.

THE TERM PAPER AMENDMENT

The Twenty-seventh Amendment says that when Congress votes to give its members a raise, they will not receive it until the following term. The point is to discourage congresspeople from raising their own salaries as soon as they're elected. This was originally the second of twelve proposed amendments, ten of which became the Bill of Rights. James Madison introduced it in 1789, but it was not approved.

In 1982, Gregory Watson, a student at the University of Texas at Austin who was researching a term paper, found a reference to this nearly forgotten proposal in a dusty library book. He abandoned his original topic—the Equal Rights Amendment—and wrote about congressional salaries instead. But he didn't stop there.

Watson started a letter-writing campaign—typewritten letters, since desktop computers and the internet didn't exist yet—to drum up support around the country to pass this amendment. For the next ten years, he said, he "would eat, drink, sleep and breath [sic] the ratification of the amendment." He succeeded, and Michigan became the thirty-eighth state to ratify it in May 1992.

Watson had received a grade of C on his paper for his fanciful suggestion that Madison's idea could still be ratified 193 years later. But you could say that he got an A for Amendment in real life. In fact, in 2017, his professor, Sharon Waite, changed his grade to A+.

Some states would ratify the Constitution as long as the new Congress made adding amendments that guaranteed fundamental rights the first order of business. Congress did so, and the Bill of Rights was quickly ratified by 1791.

Since then, only seventeen amendments have been added—and none since 1992.

To change the Constitution, you have to play offense, and the rules are complicated. So far, all amendments have been proposed by Congress, which involves getting support from two-thirds of the members of both the House and the Senate.

This is no small task. To adopt a proposed amendment by this method, you need 67 out of 100 senators plus 288 of the 435 members of the House of Representatives (assuming everyone is present and voting).

Or, if that seems too difficult, you could try to get two-thirds of the states to sign petitions and force Congress to call a new Constitutional Convention. The hitch is that a majority of *both* the upper and lower houses of thirty-four of the fifty states have to agree. This method has never occurred, although what turned into the Seventeenth Amendment came close.

But holding a convention is no guarantee that any particular proposal will be agreed to or even considered. That's because, once it is called, the convention can do whatever it wants— or nothing at all. Moreover, given that all a convention can do is *propose*

WOULD YOU LIKE TO HELP PASS AN AMENDMENT TO THE CONSTITUTION?

THE CHILD LABOR AMENDMENT WOULD PROTECT WORKERS – UNDER THE AGE OF 18. –

CONGRESS APPROVED THIS AMENDMENT IN **1924,** BUT IT HAS NO TIME LIMIT FOR RATIFICATION BY THE STATES.

BY 1937, 28 STATES HAD APPROVED IT

YOU JUST NEED TO COLLECT 10 MORE STATES AND IT WILL BECOME LAW

amendments, one quarter of the states plus one—thirteen—could torpedo any efforts at change.

Let's say that, by one route or the other, your amendment is officially under consideration. Now it must be ratified. There are two ways to do that. Most likely you'll need the approval of both houses of the legislature in three-quarters of the states. That amounts

THE UNIQUE TWENTY-FIRST AMENDMENT

The Twenty-first Amendment repealed the Eighteenth, which prohibited the manufacture, sale, transportation, and importation of "intoxicating liquors." Supporters of the repeal feared temperance unions would persuade state legislators to back down. So they called for state ratifying conventions. In less than a year, thirty-six of the forty-eight states voted for repeal.

to at least seventy-five chambers in at least thirty-eight states. (This assumes that one of the states is Nebraska, with its unicameral, or single, house. Should Nebraska not approve of an amendment, then you will need a total of seventy-six houses in the same thirty-eight states to win.) Or Congress can designate state-ratifying conventions as the method by which the amendment is voted on. Again, three-quarters of the states must approve. This has happened only once, with the Twenty-first Amendment.

Blocking an amendment is far easier than backing one. You have two options.

• Persuade one-third of the members plus one more in either house of Congress to vote against it.

• Or get one legislative house in thirteen states to vote against ratification. The Illinois legislature requires a three-fifths supermajority to approve constitutional amendments. The ERA came up every year between 1972 and 1982. Some years it passed the House; other years, the Senate—but never both in the same year. Illinois did not adopt the ERA.

Even a successful amendment can take an agonizingly long time to become official. Consider the Nineteenth Amendment, which gave women the vote. The first measure was introduced in Congress in 1878. Nine years passed before the proposal even got out of committee. Then the Senate voted it down. Forty-one years later, in 1919, Congress finally approved the amendment, although not until after President Woodrow Wilson called a rare special session of Congress to nudge it through the Senate.

Ratification required agreement of thirty-six of the forty-eight states then in the union. Tennessee became the last state to ratify the Nineteenth Amendment. The vote in the Tennessee House of Representatives amounted to fifty in favor and forty-nine opposed. Had one representative changed his vote, the amendment would have failed.

Many—possibly most—Americans agree with the process Madison designed. The Constitution should not be easy to change. Otherwise it might become "clogged," as one Framer said, with requirements.

But making the Constitution nearly impossible to amend is good only if it is not flawed.

There are Other Ways
States

Processes to revise state constitutions vary widely.

Florida has more ways to amend its constitution than any other state. Every

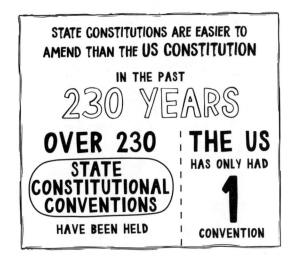

twenty years, an appointed commission can propose changes. The legislature and Constitutional Conventions can also do so. Ordinary citizens can use an initiative process. And a Tax and Budget Commission can recommend revisions to taxes.

Eighteen states allow the public to propose and then vote on amendments as an initiative-and-referendum process. Fourteen states allow the electorate to decide whether to call a Constitutional Convention on a scheduled basis. New York, for instance, does so every twenty years—and in 2017 voted not to do so. The last time Oklahoma allowed citizens to vote on a convention, however, was in 1970.

All fifty states allow their legislatures to propose amendments, though they follow different procedures. All except Delaware then require that the electorate ratify any proposed amendments.

Other Countries

No other country has a constitution so difficult to amend as that of the United States. In Sweden and Austria, the parliament can amend the constitution as easily as it passes laws. Argentina, France, Ireland, and Norway, among other countries, require more complex procedures; nevertheless, the legislatures have the power to add amendments.

A number of other countries require referenda—votes by the electorate—to change their constitutions. Australia, for example, begins its process if an absolute majority of the House and Senate agree, but the Australian electorate makes the final decision. A majority of Australians and a majority of the six states have to acquiesce. This and other provisions make the Australian constitution difficult to amend.

Several countries' constitutions absolutely prohibit changing some of their provisions through what are called "immutability" provisions or "eternity clauses." Germany, for instance, forbids changing "human dignity" as the guiding principle of its constitution.

The United States

Our country might be better off if our Constitution were easier to amend, more like states' constitutions. A number of the fault lines we've discussed could be—perhaps already could have been—corrected if that were the case.

Of course, revising the portion of the Constitution that covers the amendment process would require an amendment. Maybe this would be desirable if, as in Germany, certain provisions, such as freedom of speech, were off-limits.

The Story Continues

Congress granted the ERA an extension until June 30, 1982; however, no additional states ratified the amendment.

Schlafly won. She celebrated her victory by hosting a party for 1,100 people, at which she said, "The ERA dies tonight, morally and constitutionally."

IS IT TOO LATE?

In 2017, thirty-five years after the Equal Rights Amendment's deadline, the Nevada Assembly ratified the ERA. So did the State of Illinois in 2018. Virginia's General Assembly considered doing so, too, but in 2019, Republicans in the House of Delegates killed the measure. If another state steps up to become the thirty-eighth—the minimum needed for final approval—will the ERA become the twenty-eighth amendment? Nobody knows. Supporters argue that, since Article V of the Constitution doesn't include a time limit, it was unconstitutional for Congress to impose one as it did for the ERA in 1972. Opponents counter that a law is a law.

PART VIII
Keeping Pace with the Times

The Framers' Constitution didn't remain intact for long. Shortly after signing it and sending it out for public discussion, Alexander Hamilton wrote that ordinary Americans had the opportunity to participate in "reflection and choice" about how they wished to be governed. The First Congress took him up on that offer in 1789 by proposing the series of amendments that came to be called the Bill of Rights.

We believe that, in order to perfect the union, "reflection and choice" should be an ongoing process. And we hope you've been thinking about the Constitution's fault lines as you've read this book. The next steps ask you to accept Hamilton's invitation and follow the First Congress's example by taking part in

- reflection on how well the Constitution meets its goals, as laid out in the Preamble; and
- decisions about what to change and how.

We'll kick off the conversation, but it is up to you to offer your own "reflection(s)" and suggest your own "choice(s)" about the issues involved.

CHAPTER 21

Grading the Constitution

When Supreme Court Justice Ruth Bader Ginsburg visited Egypt in 2012, she landed in hot water with politicians and newscasters back home. Egypt's leaders were trying to reform its government, and an interviewer asked her if they should examine constitutions from around the world for ideas.

She answered yes but added, "I would not look to the U.S. Constitution, if I were drafting a Constitution in the year 2012." It was too old, she said, not likely to be at all so helpful as, say, the South African Constitution that was drafted in 1994. In any case, she explained, "We are still forming the more perfect union."

Ginsburg was criticized for being unpatriotic. If she didn't like the document that established the Supreme Court, several critics suggested, she should find another job.

❧ ❧

"Is it too much for a United States Supreme Court Justice to have a little reverence for the Constitution of the United States?"

—Glenn Beck

❧ ❧

Ginsburg's views, however, were similar to those of the Framers. They, too, believed that Americans would forever need to perfect the union, changing the Constitution along the way.

So which is the Constitution: a work that should be revered or one that is out of date? Or both?

The Preamble sets out the Framers' goals for the budding United States. To what extent does the Constitution meet their goals? Looking at the document's track record—its successes and problems—in each area allows us to give it a grade. You can do the same.

"Form a More Perfect Union"

The Framers' most basic aim was to transform the people who thought of their state as their country into citizens of the United States.

We certainly have a more perfect union than we did in 1787. Americans, by and large

- obey laws passed by the Congress the Framers created;
- pay federal taxes;
- celebrate Independence Day, put their hands over their hearts while pledging allegiance to the American flag; and

IT'S HAPPENED ELSEWHERE. COULD IT HAPPEN HERE?

In 2014, 45 percent of Scots voted for their country to secede from Great Britain, which has existed since 1709. Over 70 percent of voters aged sixteen and seventeen supported the idea. Since 55 percent overall preferred to stay, it didn't happen.

However, in 2016, 52 percent of people living in Great Britain voted for "Brexit," withdrawing from the European Union. That process is underway. In reaction, Scotland, which voted against Brexit, threatened to withdraw from Great Britain.

- vote in national elections—though not enough people do so.

All of these acts indicate respect for and attachment to the union.

On the other hand, many aspects of the Constitution produce problems as well as pride. Our bicameral system, the presidential veto, and supermajority requirements for overcoming Senate filibusters make it very difficult to pass new and necessary laws. This gridlock has led many Americans to lose faith in government, especially Congress.

Fracturing into separate realms was a threat in 1787. Less than seventy-five years later, America went to war against itself to prevent Southern states from seceding; 750,000 people lost their lives in the Civil War. This slaughter has discouraged further efforts at secession. But can we be confident that no state will ever want to split off?

In a 2008 survey, 40 percent of young people between the ages of eighteen and twenty-nine suggested that their states should secede and form their own countries. In 2014, about a quarter of the US population agreed. By 2017, a third of Californians supported withdrawing from the union. And, Texas Boys State passed a bill asserting, "For God and Country, The Republic of Texas hereby Declares her Independence."

Increasingly, states are defined as being either red or blue because a large majority of the residents are either Republicans or Democrats. Increasingly, they seem to distrust and even express contempt for states of the other color.

That's a lot of people unhappy with the federal government and a lot of states riled up with each other.

FORM A MORE PERFECT UNION	C−

"Establish Justice"

The Constitution created a system of federal courts that has often protected people's rights, as the Framers intended.

There are many examples of ways in which the Constitution, especially as amended, has succeeded in establishing—or at least seeking—justice:

• Article VI says that elected and appointed officeholders can be any religion.

• Amendments finally overturned slavery, the Fugitive Slave Clause, and other atrocious provisions.

• Decisions by federal courts that overrule states' voter ID laws and gerrymandering practices show that these courts can help establish justice.

Many of these issues, though, are complicated. After all, a majority of the people's representatives in some state legislatures voted in favor of ID laws and congressional districts with weird shapes. They probably think the courts' decisions are unjust because they overturned the will of the people. There are debates, too, about whether courts should have any say over how states determine congressional boundaries.

Americans' definitions of "justice" have broadened since 1787, but we don't agree on the specifics any more than the Framers did. Most citizens believe that access to affordable health care is a right; many others dispute that.

By not including national guidelines for elections in the Constitution, the Framers allowed states to develop inconsistent rules, some of which limit citizens' ability to vote. The provision that assigns two senators to every state, regardless of its size, is unfair. So is the one that makes the Constitution so difficult to amend. Is justice always done

when the president pardons someone convicted of a crime?

Above all, the processes for nominating and confirming both judges to preside over our federal courts and the Attorney General of the United States have been severely questioned.

Even if new laws could help resolve some of these issues—well, you've seen how hard it is to get bills through Congress. If the Constitution allowed direct democracy, Americans might be able to overturn or work around some of these hardwired problems. But it doesn't.

ESTABLISH JUSTICE	C

"Insure Domestic Tranquility"

To the Framers, domestic tranquility meant that people could work and raise families without being distracted by political bitterness or violent uprisings. Over time, the Constitution did help resolve the issues they faced. Here are some developments:

- Farmers no longer raid munitions depots as Daniel Shays' followers did.
- Enslaved persons don't rebel because chattel slavery was repealed.
- States agree on the locations of their borders.

Americans in general have enjoyed periods of tranquility, though minority groups and poor people have often felt ignored and even oppressed. In the nineteenth century, the government forcibly displaced Native Americans. In the 1950s and 1960s, cities' attempts to prevent desegregation triggered mass demonstrations. Urban riots in poverty-stricken neighborhoods and protests against America's involvement in the Vietnam War also roiled the country, sometimes violently. Governors and President Lyndon B. Johnson used armed force to suppress them.

The country quieted down for several decades. Then the deaths of African Americans at the hands of police sparked more demonstrations. Native Americans opposed a government plan to lay an oil pipeline across the Standing Rock reservation. About three million people—roughly 1 percent of the US population—took to the streets to protest the inauguration of President Donald J. Trump in early 2017, and actions persist, including marches, lawsuits, and investigations.

Furthermore, many people remain distressed and at odds with one another about

- race relations;
- the meaning of religious freedom;
- the place of guns in society;
- immigration; and
- the possibility of terrorism, both homegrown and foreign.

In addition, many Americans express dissatisfaction with Congress and other government institutions. And political elections, including the 2016 presidential campaign and the 2018 midterms, seem even more bitter, hostile, and contested. Our political system, including the increasingly powerful presidency, seem to be polarizing the populace rather than bringing us together. The Framers' wish to avoid factions totally failed.

INSURE DOMESTIC TRANQUILITY — C

"Provide for the Common Defense"

The Framers wrote into the Constitution that the federal government has the right to raise and support armies and to provide and maintain a navy. (Of course, an air force didn't occur to them!) The government collects taxes from the citizenry to pay for the military protection of the nation as a whole.

These steps alone improved "common defense" far beyond what could be provided under the Articles of Confederation, a time when ordinary citizens had to rely on themselves and their neighbors for protection. The United States spends more on its military than the next seven countries in the world combined and also more than all the remaining countries combined. And political leaders often proclaim, likely accurately, that we have the finest-trained armed forces in the world.

Yet because of the Senate and funding formulas that play favorites with small states, the states that need the most protection might not receive it. And Congress sometimes funds weapons programs—even ones the Pentagon opposes!—because they give jobs to constituents.

Furthermore, some types of threats might overwhelm our armed services' ability to respond. Biological weapons and telecommunications shutdowns might make a military response almost irrelevant. Climate change, too, poses threats to national security.

Since the end of World War II, common defense has involved international agreements and mutual protection among multiple countries. President Trump, however, has angered some of America's longtime allies, who might decide not to come to our defense if we are threatened. He also dismisses the Pentagon's warnings about the importance of climate change.

PROVIDE FOR THE COMMON DEFENSE — B

"Promote the General Welfare"

With their pen strokes, the Framers eliminated taxes on goods exported from one state to another and gave authority and funds to the government to build roads.

In the twenty-first century our interstate infrastructure and economic system is fully national, thanks in part to the Interstate Highway System built in the 1950s.

Even in the eighteenth century, though, leaders hoped for more, including a national rather than local frame of mind. It's possible that a federal form of government, in which states form the basis of representation in both houses of Congress, limits our ability to think about the needs of the country as a whole. How concerned are Midwesterners about rising sea levels along the Gulf Coast or fires in the West? Or farmers about urban problems—or urban dwellers about people who live in rural areas? Or many of us about the rights of persons who differ in race, religion, national origin, primary language, or sexual orientation? As wealthy Americans become wealthier, the general welfare of low-income people sinks.

Even if we do all care about one another, Congress and the other institutions established in the Constitution are having trouble resolving these issues.

PROMOTE THE GENERAL WELFARE	C—

"Secure the Blessings of Liberty to Ourselves and Our Posterity"

The Framers defined "liberty" as citizens being able to govern themselves.

We're better off in many ways than ever before. The United States is not ruled by kings or tyrants, and you don't have to be a white tax-paying male to vote or run for office.

Americans certainly have more liberties today than in 1787. Some of these result from decisions by the Supreme Court, which has interpreted "freedom of speech" in the Constitution's First Amendment to mean freedom of expression. So people can march in the streets, wave signs, even burn the flag—actions that used to be barred. People are also more free to express their gender orientation and sexuality than in the past.

On the other hand, political leaders have recently criticized protests such as marching and kneeling rather than standing while the national anthem is sung. President Trump discourages freedom of the press by referring to reports he disagrees with as "fake news." Above all, the Constitution restricts participation in government in many ways—through gerrymandering, a lack of direct democracy, limits on voting rights and running for national office, the Electoral College, habeas corpus, and preventing residents of the District of Columbia from having a voting representative in Congress.

Furthermore, unless the problems of determining continuity in government are resolved, there might not be much of a government to participate in following a devastating catastrophe.

SECURE THE BLESSINGS OF LIBERTY TO OURSELVES AND OUR POSTERITY	

The Constitution

Combining these grades—assuming they're all equally important—we give the Constitution an overall grade of C.

If you agree that fissures in the Constitution make it hard to meet the great goals set out in the Preamble, then maybe you also think that something should be done about them. From the beginning, with the almost immediate adoption of the Bill of Rights, this founding document has been a work in progress. How can we improve the Constitution?

THE CONSTITUTION'S REPORT CARD

SUBJECT	GRADE
FORM A MORE PERFECT UNION	C−
ESTABLISH JUSTICE	C
INSURE DOMESTIC TRANQUILITY	C
PROVIDE FOR THE COMMON DEFENSE	B
PROMOTE THE GENERAL WELFARE	C−
SECURE THE BLESSINGS OF LIBERTY TO OURSELVES AND OUR POSTERITY	B−
AVERAGE	**C**

CHAPTER 22

Now What?

"Improve and Perpetuate"

Some of the stories you've read in this book are downright scary. The Constitution is supposed to shield us; however, it leaves us vulnerable to injustice and possible chaos and mayhem. Those are serious fault lines.

The metaphor of fault lines comes from geology and refers to shifting tectonic plates beneath the earth's surface that can cause rumbles ranging from mild vibrations to catastrophic earthquakes and tsunamis. Architects safeguard residents in these zones by constructing buildings that can withstand shaking.

But what if you lived in a building that got a C on an earthquake safety test? Assuming you decided not to move, you'd want your home shored up. That's what we believe the Constitution needs—reinforcement. And it's up to all of us to provide it. In fact, most Americans agree: six out of ten believe that our Constitution is no better than average, compared to the constitutions of other countries. Who wants to be just average—or worse?

Even while praising the Framers for their work and urging adoption of the new Constitution, James Madison wrote, "it is incumbent on their successors to improve and perpetuate" it. The year 1787 was a beginning, not a conclusion.

We've laid out four ways to improve the Constitution. To recap...

1. Change Senate rules

To reduce congressional gridlock, the Senate could simply delete the filibuster from its rulebook and allow a majority of those present at a meeting to "call the question." This motion, which most organizations use, brings the matter under discussion to a vote.

2. Pass new laws

The difficulty of passing legislation is itself one of the fault lines. Still, Congress could cure a number of others by passing laws.

Allow multimember districts chosen by proportional representation rather than requiring single-member districts in the House of Representatives to limit or even eliminate gerrymandering. Or establish nationwide standards for the shape or composition of districts and require all states to follow them, possibly using nonpartisan commissions to draw district lines.

Admit the District of Columbia as the fifty-first state of the union to provide residents of the District with representation.

Require that every state divide its Electoral College votes proportionately, rather than giving all of them to the winner.

Create a law covering predictable misfortunes, so that the public could be confident that sound plans for presidential succession are in place.

Specify the types of emergencies that could befall the country and clarify who has authority to issue which orders.

3. Develop Work-arounds

Some fault lines can be patched up creatively.

The Electoral College could be defanged if the eleven largest states agreed to cast their electoral votes for whoever came in first in the national vote. If they refused, then any combination of at least one large state plus enough smaller states to add up to 270

Electoral College votes could reach the same result.

To clarify the reasons for presidential pardons, the Department of Justice or an independent board could review and comment on them.

Congress should consider which high-level government officials should be subject to confirmation by the Senate—not simply appointed by the president.

4. Amend the Constitution

Hard as it is to accomplish, repairing most fault lines requires amending the Constitution in order to solve some problems.

Break the ability of both houses of Congress to veto each other's bills by providing ways for some bills to become law even if they cannot procure a majority in both.

Make the voting power in the Senate proportional to the size of each state's population.

Increase the number of senators while keeping the voting power equal.

Revise the ability of the president to veto legislation, including making it easier for Congress to override vetoes.

Specify that the Senate must follow majority rule for other issues in addition to ratifying treaties, proposing amendments, and convicting a federal official who has been impeached by the House of Representatives.

Give citizens ways to affect laws directly, without having to go through Congress.

Eliminate or revise age and citizenship requirements for office-seekers, including those for the presidency.

Allow presidents to serve more than two terms under certain circumstances.

End a president's term early through a vote of no confidence by Congress or a recall vote by the electorate.

Replace the Electoral College with a system that would require that the winner achieve a majority either in the initial election or in a runoff between the top two candidates.

Clarify how and under what circumstances to replace deceased or incapacitated public officials.

Fill in the details of who takes over the presidency and under what circumstances.

Allow sitting members of Congress to serve in the cabinet without having to give up their legislative seats.

Reduce the gap between election and inauguration days, assuming the Electoral College is eliminated.

Specify if and when rights, such as freedom of the press, can be suspended in times of congressionally declared emergencies.

Allow Congress—or the president—to suspend habeas corpus in situations besides rebellion or invasion.

Make it easier to amend the Constitution, either by reducing the votes required to propose or ratify amendments or by allowing direct proposal and ratification by the electorate.

That's a lot of amendments! Taken together, they would transform much of our governmental system and processes as we know them—perhaps necessarily.

It is very difficult to get even a popular amendment through the grueling approval process. So far, all twenty-seven successful amendments began, like the ERA, in Congress.

But there's another way to trigger discussion about changes to the Constitution: hold another Constitutional Convention.

At the state level, that's happened over two hundred and thirty times. At the national level, it's occurred only once, in Philadelphia.

If two-thirds of the states petition Congress to call such a convention, then Congress "shall"—that's lawyerese for "must"—call one. Or Congress itself could do the honors.

A Constitutional Convention?!

At this point, "We-the-authors" part ways, at least in this book, in our points of view about a convention. Just as the Framers debated the original document, we'll share our debate with you.

Sandy: Most Americans don't connect the dots from what's happening in their lives—including what's in their food—

to the Constitution. They have no idea how dangerous the Constitution is. And what's really bad is that people get angry at politicians they don't like—or place excessive faith in those they do—without realizing that many of the government's failures result from limitations in the Constitution rather than the defects of individual leaders.

Cynthia: But why a convention? That's such a drastic suggestion. We could get a lot done simply by changing the rules, putting some work-arounds in place, and passing laws.

Sandy: But it's the Constitution that makes it harder and harder for legislation to succeed. Moreover, as you and I agree, in many cases amendments are necessary. The question is whether we can trust Congress to step up and propose the amendments we need. I have no confidence that they can and will. Members of Congress protect their own political interests—so that some might oppose eliminating gerrymandering

that benefits them personally, for instance. And they're not even willing to face the possibility of a massive attack and state clearly who's going to lead the country in the aftermath.

Cynthia: All of that is true. However, once you open the Constitution to wholesale revisions, there's no knowing what might happen. A convention could erase the Bill of Rights. We could end up returning to a president and vice president from different parties or we could have a House of Representatives with five thousand members. Convention-eers might eliminate half of the president's cabinet—and the services those agencies provide, like food programs for Americans in need.

Sandy: If we believe in government by the people, that's the risk we have to take. But I'm more optimistic than you are. Though we discuss a few rights, like habeas corpus and freedom of speech, this book concentrates almost totally on the *structures* established by the

1787 Constitution. If we ever had the kind of convention I want, almost all of the discussion would focus on those structures. People are calmer when they're talking about structures—where there aren't obvious winners and losers—than when they are arguing about rights.

Cynthia: People are not necessarily calmer when talking about structures. Those who live in the forty-one states with relatively low populations would not graciously relinquish one of their senators to a larger state like California or New York. Anyway, you can't control the agenda at a Constitutional Convention. You couldn't order people to leave the amendments alone. Look what the Framers did to the Articles of Confederation.

Sandy: If people start shouting about their favorite (or least favorite) rights, then a "runaway" convention would break up, as almost happened in 1787 over voting power in the Senate. I'm confident that the country wouldn't stand for repealing the Bill of Rights. I believe that "we the people" are capable of "reflection and choice."

Cynthia: I agree with you in principle. But, just trying to call for a convention could cause a crisis. How would the delegates be chosen? Who would make the rules—Congress or the delegates? Would we follow the one-state/one-vote rule, like in 1787? Or would we demand proportional voting? Delaware would never allow that.

Sandy: These are good questions, to which we don't have answers. That provision—Article V—is probably my least favorite part of the Constitution. It provides no clue how to run a convention. I wish the Framers had called for a convention every twenty-five years.

Cynthia: But, they didn't. And, Congress has incentive to call for a convention, which would change how Congress is selected and operates.

Sandy: If Congress doesn't call a convention, two-thirds of the states can petition to call one. If there's a groundswell of support for the idea, it could happen. As of 2019, there are actually quite a few people who take this option seriously. If a new convention happens, it will be because millions of Americans realize there really are fault lines that need to be fixed before some kind of political earthquake destroys our government's ability to function.

Cynthia: If there's that much interest in changing the Constitution, then I believe the people's representatives in Congress *would* propose the amendments we need. And the states would ratify them. I'm sticking with the amendment route.

Sandy: And I believe we need a Constitutional Convention.

Cynthia and Sandy: But, like the Framers, we can agree on a compromise.

SPEAK UP!

Throughout the Constitutional Convention, the Framers held straw votes on the issues they debated. These votes didn't count; they weren't official. But they gave the delegates a chance to express their opinions at a given moment and then change their minds without committing themselves or the country to a final decision.

In the same way, America could hold straw conventions—discussions of the Constitution's fault lines, which ones are the most pressing, and what to do about them.

You can take part. In fact, you can help get the conversation started. When you hear people say that they don't trust the government or that Congress doesn't seem able to fix big problems like immigration—tell them it's the Constitution's fault! Then explain how, banding together, we can repair it. That would make us a true union. And when you're old enough, make *your* vote count.

TIMELINE OF KEY EVENTS CITED IN
FAULT LINES IN THE CONSTITUTION

Date	Event / Chapters
1774–1781	First and Second Continental Congresses convene. *Introduction*
July 4, 1776	Colonists issue the Declaration of Independence. *Introduction*
1776–1781	The Revolutionary War is fought, ending at the Battle of Yorktown. *Introduction*
1781–1789	The Articles of Confederation and Perpetual Union are in effect. *Introduction* Confederation Congress convenes in a series of locations. *Introduction*
1783	Soldiers storm Confederation Congress for back pay. *Introduction*
1786	Shays' Rebellion occurs. *Introduction*
1787	Confederation Congress approves Constitutional Convention. *Introduction*
May 25–September 17, 1787	Constitutional Convention is held in Philadelphia. *All*
1787–1788	Ratification debates and conventions are held around the country. *Preamble, 4, 18* The Federalist is written and distributed. *Preamble*
March 1789	First US Congress convenes. *3, 17, 18, 19*
April 30, 1789	George Washington is inaugurated. *6*
December 1791	Congress proposes and states ratify the Bill of Rights. *18, 20*
1794	Albert Gallatin is found ineligible to serve in the US Senate. *9*
1794–1795	Farmers in Pennsylvania protest taxes during the Whiskey Rebellion. President Washington pardons them. *13*
1796	Political parties begin to form. President John Adams and Vice President Thomas Jefferson belong to different parties. *1, 12*
1801	The House of Representatives names Jefferson president. *12*
1804	Twelfth Amendment is ratified, clarifying rules for presidential electors. *12*
1812	Elbridge Gerry gerrymanders a Massachusetts congressional district. *5*
1825	The House of Representatives names John Quincy Adams president, even though Andrew Jackson received more popular votes. *12*

1842	Congress adopts the Apportionment Act, requiring single-member Congressional districts. *5*
1861	Supreme Court rules that President Abraham Lincoln cannot suspend habeas corpus. *19*
1861–1865	The Civil War is fought. *8, 9, 17, 19, 21*
1865	President Andrew Johnson pardons Confederates. *13*
1868	Fourteenth Amendment is ratified, guaranteeing "equal protection of the laws." *2, 8, 9, 19, 20*
1870	Fifteenth Amendment is ratified, prohibiting states from restricting voting on the basis of race. *8*
1870	Hiram Revels becomes first African-American US senator. *9*
1888	Benjamin Harrison becomes president, even though Grover Cleveland won more popular votes. *12*
1913	Richard Puckett is lynched in South Carolina. *1* Senate adopts Rule XXII regarding filibuster. *4*
1913	Seventeenth Amendment is ratified, giving citizens, rather than state legislatures, the right to vote for senator. *15*
1914–1918	The Great War (World War I) is fought. *18*
1918	Eugene V. Debs is sentenced to prison under the Espionage Act of 1917. *17*
1918	Representative Leonidas C. Dyer introduces first antilynching legislation. *1*
1920	Nineteenth Amendment is ratified, giving women the right to vote. *8, 20*
1930s to present	Congress passes farm bills that favor certain crops. *2*
1933	Twentieth Amendment is ratified, moving Inauguration Day from March 4 to January 20. *17*
1939–1945	World War II is fought. *11, 15, 17, 18*
1940	Franklin Delano Roosevelt runs for president for an unprecedented third time and wins. He wins again in 1944. *11*
1942	After Japanese forces bomb Pearl Harbor, President Roosevelt orders internment of Japanese-Americans. *11*
1944	The Supreme Court rules against Fred Korematsu, declaring the president can limit some civil rights during wartime. *18*
1951	Twenty-second Amendment is ratified, limiting the president to two terms. *11*
1961	Twenty-third Amendment is ratified, giving residents of the District of Columbia the right to vote for president. *5*

1964	Supreme Court declares "little federalism" unconstitutional. *2*
1964	Twenty-fourth Amendment is ratified, prohibiting poll taxes to limit the right to vote. *8*
1967	Twenty-fifth Amendment is ratified, listing the presidential order of succession. *16*
1972–1982	Phyllis Schlafly protests ratification of the Equal Rights Amendment. *20*
1971	Twenty-sixth Amendment is ratified, giving eighteen-year-olds the right to vote. *8*
1972–1974	Burglars working for the committee to reelect President Richard M. Nixon break into the Democrats' headquarters in the Watergate. Nixon tries to fire the special prosecutor, triggering the Saturday Night Massacre. Nixon resigns. Vice President Gerald Ford becomes president and pardons Nixon. *13*
1977	President Jimmy Carter pardons men who emigrated to Canada to avoid the draft. *13*
1981	President Ronald Reagan is shot. *16*
1992	President George W. Bush sends troops to Somalia a month before President Bill Clinton's inauguration. *17* President Bush pardons people involved in the Iran-Contra Affair. *13*
1992	Spurred by Gregory Watson, the Twenty-seventh Amendment is ratified, preventing congresspeople from giving themselves an immediate raise. *20*
2000	The Supreme Court declares Governor George W. Bush the winner of the presidential election, even though Al Gore Jr. received more popular votes. *12*
September 11, 2001	Al Qaeda terrorists attack the World Trade Center, the Pentagon, and a United Airlines flight. *2, 15*
2001	Congress adopts USA PATRIOT Act. *2*
2003–2017	The Texas Legislature redraws the state's congressional districts. *5*
2005	US Senate adopts Resolution 39 apologizing for lynchings. *1*
2006	Michigan's Proposal 2, started by Jennifer Gratz, bans affirmative action at public institutions. *7*
2007	President George W. Bush vetoes SCHIP. *3*
2008	Senator John McCain, born in Panama Canal Zone, runs for president. *10*
December 2010	Leezia Dhalla learns she is undocumented. The DREAM Act fails to achieve the necessary supermajority vote in the Senate. *4*

2011	Mayor Vincent Gray is arrested for protesting Taxation without Representation in Washington, DC. *6*
2014	Kaci Hickox is quarantined in New Jersey against her will after treating patients with Ebola in Sierra Leone. *19*
2015	Mary Lou Miller is prevented from voting in San Antonio, Texas. *8*
2016	Donald J. Trump becomes president, even though Hillary Rodham Clinton won more popular votes. *12*
2017–2018	President Trump fires James B. Comey, Director of the Federal Bureau of Investigation, as well as Secretary of State Rex Tillerson and Attorney General Jeff Sessions. *14*
2019	President Trump declares an emergency regarding undocumented immigrants at the US–Mexico border and vetoes Congress's override. *19*

ACKNOWLEDGMENTS

We are deeply grateful to the following scholars, colleagues, friends, and family members for generously sharing their expertise:

Paul Finkelman on the early configuration of the states and on the Constitutional Convention; Jack Rakove on the meanings of the Preamble; Cynthia Leitich-Smith on indigenous Nations; Charles Papirmeister on the USA PATRIOT Act; Frances Lee on the Senate; Anne Dunkelberg and Joan Aiker on SCHIP; Leezia Dahla, Claudia Yoli, and Michael Churgin on US immigration policy and practice; Michael Mucchetti and Michael Li on gerrymandering; Bradley Truding and Ariel Levinson-Waldman on Washington, DC; Beth Stevens and Emma Weinstein-Levy on voting rights; Victor Ferreres on voting in Spain; Elizabeth Goitein on emergency powers; Marc Lipsitch, Susan Murrow, and James Hodge on public health and epidemics; Rachel Levinson-Waldman on cyber-threats; Meira Levinson on civics education; and H. W. Brands and Michael Stoff for historical background.

University of Texas School of Law students Francesca Eick, Barbara dePeña, Bruce Baldree, and Savannah Kumar provided invaluable research assistance, and Trish Do met all our logistical needs.

Cynthia's critique partners Vicki Coe, Cheryl Lawton Malone, and Patrice Sherman in Boston, and Shelley Jackson and Janice Shefelman in Austin asked all the right questions and raised understandable doubts. Ella Lipsitch and Rebecca Lipsitch, too, critiqued without mercy. Ted McConnell and Maeva Marcus enthusiastically read a draft and saved us from mortifying errors.

This project was the unlikely brainchild of Kathy Landwehr, our imaginative and probing editor. We hope we have done her and Margaret Quinlin proud and appreciate the opportunity to update the information for this edition. Cheers to Nicki Carmack and Adela Pons for their eye-catching design. Erin Murphy, in response to your completely reasonable question, yes, we can apparently have both a marriage and a book.

Almost every family member was integrally involved in this one, and all remain as thoroughly splendid as ever.

NOTES

INTRODUCTION
Page

8   "Virginia, Sir, is my country": James West Davidson, William E. Gienapp, Christine Leigh Heyrman, Mark H Lytle, and Michael B. Stoff, *Nation of Nations: A Narrative History of the American Republic* (Boston: McGraw Hill, 2005), p. 196

8   "Massachusetts is our country": ibid.

8   "It is...of government": Joy Hakim, *From Colonies to Country, 1735–1791* (New York: Oxford University Press, 2003), p. 137

9   "imbecility" Federalist No. 15

10   "I predict...every step": James West Davidson and Michael B. Stoff, *The American Nation* (Upper Saddle River: Prentice Hall, 2004), p. 204

10   "Influence is...be secured": Richard Beeman, *Plain, Honest Men: The Making of the American Constitution* (New York: Random House, 2009), p. 17

11   "an assembly of demi-gods": Letter from Thomas Jefferson to John Adams, Paris, August 30, 1787. *www.founders.archives.gov/documents/Jefferson/01-12-02-0075*

PREAMBLE
Page

13   "We the...our Posterity": Beeman, *Plain, Honest Men*, p. 347

14   "I wish...the states": Mr. Joseph Taylor, North Carolina Ratifying Convention, 24 July 1788. Philip B. Kurland and Ralph Lerner, editors, *The Founders' Constitution, Volume 2. http://press-pubs.uchicago.edu/founders/tocs/toc.html*

16   "we may...divided people": Peter Charles Hoffer, *For Ourselves and Our Posterity: The Preamble to the Federal Constitution in American History* (Oxford: Oxford University Press, 2012), p. 33

19   "Resolved that...said legislature": Continental Congress, April 1, 1779, Resolutions on Indian Raids. Image 284. George Washington Papers at the Library of Congress, 1741–1799: Series 4. General Correspondence. 1697–1799. *www.loc.gov/item/mgw453775*

19   "The misfortune...be allowed": Letter from William Grayson to Beverley Randolph, June 25, 1787. Letters of Delegates to Congress: Volume 24, November 6, 1786–February 29, 1788, Item 79. *www.memory.loc.gov/ammem/amlaw/lwdg.html*

19   "Just imported...Ringworms, etc.": William Crosskey, *Politics and the Constitution in the History of the United States* (Chicago: The University of Chicago Press, 1953), Volume 1, p. 298

CHAPTER 1: IT TAKES TWO TO TANGO / BICAMERALISM
Page

23   "accosting a white woman": Avis Thomas-Lester, "A Senate Apology for History on Lynching," *Washington Post*, June 14, 2005. *www.washingtonpost.com/wp-dyn/content/article/2005/06/13/AR2005061301720.html*

24   "Whenever a...to die": ibid.

24   "passed over": Jeffery A. Jenkins, Justin Peck, and Vesla M. Weaver, "Between Reconstructions:

Congressional Action on Civil Rights, 1891–1940," *Studies in American Political Development,* Volume 24, April 2010, p. 54. *https://cpb-us-e1.wpmucdn.com/sites.usc.edu/dist/2/77/files/2018/01/race_SAPD-wy2y68.pdf*

27   "His style…His Excellency": Ray Raphael, *Mr. President: How and Why the Founders Created a Chief Executive* (New York: Alfred A. Knopf, 2012), pp. 93–94

27   "there were…fire companies": ibid., p. 159

27   "a more…of men": Anthony King, *The Founding Fathers v. The People: Paradoxes of American Democracy* (Cambridge: Harvard University Press, 2012), p. 37

27   "with more…popular branch": ibid., p. 44

27   "The people are…dupes": Beeman, *Plain, Honest Men*, p. 114

28   "excess of law-making": Federalist No. 62

30   "this complicated…as beneficial": Federalist No. 62

30   "there is…done twice": Nebraska Legislature: The official site of the Nebraska Unicameral Legislature. *www.nebraskalegislature.gov/about/history_unicameral.php*

31   "apologizes to…20th century": S.Res. 39 (109th): "Lynching Victims Senate Apology resolution." *www.govtrack.us/congress/bills/109/sres39/text*

32   "There may…bears responsibility": Thomas-Lester, "A Senate Apology for History on Lynching"

CHAPTER 2: BIG STATES, LITTLE SAY / THE SENATE
Page

34   "Whether it's…basic things": Amanda Ripley, "How We Got Homeland Security Wrong," *Time*, March 22, 2004. *www.cnn.com/2004/ALLPOLITICS/03/22/homesec.tm*

34   "in the…popcorn explodes": Eric Lipton, "Come One, Come All, Join the Terror Target List," *New York Times*, July 12, 2006. *http://query.nytimes.com/gst/fullpage.html?res=9505E4D61130F931A25754C0A9609C8B63*

34   "the upside-down…homeland-security funding": Ripley, "How We Got Homeland Security Wrong"

34   "We have…people in": ibid.

35   "World War…the formula": ibid.

36   "it might…the Convention": "Madison Debates, May 30, 1787." *http://avalon.law.yale.edu/18th_century/debates_530.asp*

36   "Will not…monstrous influence": "Madison Debates, June 8, 1787." *http://avalon.law.yale.edu/18th_century/debates_608.asp*

36   "injure the…the people": Beeman, *Plain, Honest Men*, p. 182

37   "I do…trust you": ibid., p. 184

37   "the small progress": Gordon Lloyd, "The Constitutional Convention," Teaching American History. *www.teachingamericanhistory.org/convention/summary*

37   "prayers imploring…of heaven": ibid.

37   "disunion, anarchy and misery": Beeman, *Plain, Honest Men*, p. 203

37   "deplorable state…the Convention": ibid., p.185

38   "If we…an end": ibid., p. 188

39   "a defeat, not [a] compromise": Jack N. Rackove, *Revolutionaries: A New History of the Invention of America* (New York: Houghton Mifflin, 2010), p. 372

39   "lesser evil": James Madison, Federalist No. 62

40   "Taxpayers are…country sick": Anahad O'Connor, "How the Government Supports Your Junk Food Habit," *New York Times*, July 19, 2016. *https://well.blogs.nytimes.com/2016/07/19/how-the-government-supports-your-junk-food-habit*

CHAPTER 3: DELETE! / PRESIDENTIAL VETO
Page

47   "the morally…to do": David Stout, "Bush Vetoes Children's Health Bill," *New York Times*, October 3, 2007. *www.nytimes.com/2007/10/03/washington/03cnd-veto.html*

47   "an irresponsible…veto pen": ibid.

47   "One of…States policy": ibid.

48   "preserve, protect…the Constitution": US Constitution, Article II, Section 1

49   "The most…ashamed of": Anthony King, *The Founding Fathers v. The People*, p. 56

CHAPTER 4: MAJORITY RULES—EXCEPT WHEN IT DOESN'T / SUPERMAJORITY RULES
Page

54   "I was…I knew": Leezia Dhalla, "'Less Than Legal': A DREAMer Awaits a Lasting Solution," *Rivard Report*, September 4, 2012. *www.therivardreport.com/less-than-legal-a-dreamer-awaits-a-lasting-solution*

55   "You don't have papers": ibid.

56   "clogged": Kurland and Lerner, *The Founders Constitution, Volume 2. http://press-pubs. uchicago.edu/founders/documents/preambles7.html*

57   "the American system… should prevail": Federalist No. 22

62   "I consider…your parents": Leezia Dhalla, personal interview, September 2, 2016

CHAPTER 5: HOW TO CHERRY-PICK VOTERS / GERRYMANDERING
Page

65   "We must…is unacceptable": Steve Bickerstaff, *Lines in the Sand: Congressional Redistricting in Texas and the Downfall of Tom DeLay* (Austin: University of Texas Press, 2010), p. 227

66   "squiggly": Matt Levin, "This Is How Efficiently Republicans Have Gerrymandered Texas Congressional Districts," *Chron*, May 6, 2015. *www.chron.com/news/politics/texas/article/This-is-how-badly-Republicans-have-gerrymandered-6246509.php#photo-710761*

66   "the Upside-Down Elephant": Christopher Ingraham, "America's Most Gerrymandered Congressional Districts," *Washington Post*, May 14, 2014. *www.washingtonpost.com/news/wonkblog/wp/2014/05/15/americas-most-gerrymandered-congressional-districts*

69   "the curse…it prevailed": "Madison Debates, August 8, 1787." *http://avalon.law.yale.edu/18th_century/debates_808.asp*

70   *"South Carolina…without slaves": David M. Kennedy, The American Spirit: United States History as Seen by Contemporaries*, Volume 1 (Boston: Wadsworth Publishing, 2015), p. 183

70   "designed for…State governments": Kurland and Lerner, *The Founders Constitution, Volume 2. http://press-pubs.uchicago.edu/founders/documents/a1_4_1s8.html*

71   "if the…[would be] excessive": Beeman, *Plain, Honest Men*, p. 282

74 "this is…national mood": Bickerstaff, *Lines in the Sand*, p. 262

74 "a blatant…congressional seats": "Gerrymandering Illinois," *Chicago Tribune*, December 27, 2011. *www.chicagotribune.com/opinion/ct-xpm-2011-12-27-ct-edit-remap-1227-jm-20111227-story.html*

75 "blood spatter…crime scene": Jeff Guo, "Welcome to America's Most Gerrymandered District," *New Republic*, November 8, 2012. *www.newrepublic.com/article/109938/marylands-3rd-district-americas-most-gerrymandered-c-district*

75 "a strategy…can compete": National Democratic Redistricting Committee. *www.democraticredistricting.com/about/#tab3*

77 "a model…the nation": Tracy Jan, "Iowa Keeping Partisanship off the Map," *Boston Globe*, December 8, 2013, p. A17. *www.bostonglobe.com/news/politics/2013/12/08/iowa-redistricting-takes-partisanship-out-mapmaking/efehCnJvNtLMIAFSQ8gp7I/story.html*

CHAPTER 6: TAXATION WITHOUT REPRESENTATION / THE DISTRICT OF COLUMBIA
Page

80 "Free DC…it anymore": John Bresnahan and Jake Sherman. "D.C. Mayor Arrested and Released," *Politico*, April 11, 2011. *www.politico.com/story/2011/04/dc-mayor-arrested-and-released-052966*

80 "unlawful assembly…of Columbia": NBC4 Washington, April 11, 2011. *www.nbcwashington.com/news/local/Mayor-Council-Members-Arrested-in-Budget-Protest-119634139.html*

81 "All we…own money": ibid.

82 "They can…they want.'" Ben Paviour, "The 52-State Strategy: The Case for D.C.," *Washington Monthly*, July / August 2018. *www.washingtonmonthly.com/magazine/july-august-2018/political-capital*

84 "Although I…our country": "Testimony of Yolanda O. Lee, U.S. Army Guard Captain, District of Columbia National Guard," "District of Columbia House Voting Rights Act of 2009, Hearing Before the Subcommittee on the Constitution, Civil Rights, and Civil Liberties of the Committee on the Judiciary, House of Representatives, One Hundred Eleventh Congress, First Session, on H. R. 157, January 27, 2009." *www.govinfo.gov/content/pkg/CHRG-111hhrg46817/html/CHRG-111hhrg46817.htm*

85 "heartbreaking": ibid.

85 "Statehood remains…Senate seats": Aaron C. Davis, "The District Is About to Declare Its Independence—from Congress," *Washington Post*, April 14, 2016. *www.washingtonpost.com/local/dc-politics/the-district-gets-ready-to-declare-independence--from-congress/2016/04/14/bc61776c-00d4-11e6-b823-707c79ce3504_story.html?utm_term=.d299f244b201*

CHAPTER 7: I'LL JUST DO IT MYSELF!—OH NO YOU WON'T / DIRECT DEMOCRACY
Page

89 "public institutions…national origin": "September 2006 Ballot Proposal 06-2: An Overview, Prepared by Suzanne Lowe, Senate Fiscal Agency." *www.senate.michigan.gov/sfa/publications/ballotprops/proposal06-2.pdf.*

89 "total exclusion…any share": Federalist No. 63

91 "pure democracy…15,000 years": Timothy Williams, "First Came a Flood of Ballot Measures from Voters. Then Politicians Pushed Back," *New York Times*, October 15, 2018. *www.nytimes.com/2018/10/15/us/referendum-initiative-legislature-dakota.html*

CHAPTER 8: WHO CAN VOTE? HOW DO YOU KNOW? / VOTING RIGHTS
Page

94   "I could…Election Day": Mary Lou Miller, "Photo ID Not That Easy to Obtain," *San Antonio Express-News*, June 12, 2015. *www.mysanantonio.com/opinion/commentary/article/Photo-ID-not-that-easy-to-obtain-6324060.php*

94   "My vote…who cannot": ibid.

CHAPTER 9: WHO GETS TO REPRESENT YOU? / RESTRICTIONS ON RUNNING FOR CONGRESS
Page

106   "some of…richest rogues": Beeman, *Plain, Honest Men*, p. 280

106   "let foreigners…for us": ibid., p. 281

106   "weaned from…and education": Federalist No. 62

106   "an emigrant…South Carolina": Beeman, *Plain, Honest Men*, p. 281

107   "reasonable limitations": Federalist No. 52

107   "greater extent…of character": Federalist No. 62

110   "If I…a success": Nicole Goodkind, "Vermont Primary: 14-Year-Old Ethan Sonneborn Wins More Than 8 Percent of Votes in Democratic Governor Primary," *Newsweek*, August 15, 2018. *www.newsweek.com/vermont-primary-election-14-year-old-sonneborn-1073047*

110   "Please go…the process": Jack Bergeson for Kansas Governor, *www.facebook.com/bergeson2018*

CHAPTER 10: WHO GETS A SHOT AT THE OVAL OFFICE? / RESTRICTIONS ON RUNNING FOR PRESIDENT
Page

112   "I just…to do": Julie Kliegman, "Reminder: John McCain Refused an Early Release from Prison Camp," *The Week*, July 18, 2015. *www.theweek.com/speedreads/567269/reminder-john-mccain-refused-early-release-from-prison-camp*

113   "brilliant appearances…as dazzle": Federalist No. 64

113   "should continue…national concerns": ibid.

114   "the commander…born citizen": Jay Wexler, *The Odd Clauses: Understanding the Constitution through Ten of Its Most Curious Provisions* (Boston: Beacon Press, 2011), p. 83

CHAPTER 11: TIME'S UP! / PRESIDENTIAL TERM LIMITS
Page

119   "An unwritten Constitution": Akhil Reed Amar, *America's Unwritten Constitution* (New York: Random House, 2005), pp. 353–355

119   "If Great…a gun": Franklin D. Roosevelt, "Fireside Chat," December 29, 1940, American Presidency Project. *www.presidency.ucsb.edu/documents/fireside-chat-9*

119   "America wants…wants Roosevelt": Susan Dunn, 1940: *FDR, Willkie, Lindbergh, Hitler—the Election Amid the Storm* (New Haven: Yale University Press, 2013), p. 138

119   "voice from the sewers": James L. Merriner, "Chicago's Political Conventions: From the 'smoke-filled' room to 'the whole world is watching'," *Illinois Issues*, August 1996. *www.lib.niu.edu/1996/ii960812.html*

119   "This is…ordinary time": Eleanor Roosevelt, "Address to the 1940 Democratic Convention," July 18, 1940. *www2.gwu.edu/~erpapers/teachinger/q-and-a/q22-erspeech.cfm*

121	"an elected monarch": Beeman, *Plain, Honest Men*, p. 169
121	"good behavior": ibid., p. 233
121	"This is…good government": ibid.
121	"it was…a King": ibid., p. 248
124	"The Judges…good Behaviour": US Constitution, Article III, Section 1

CHAPTER 12: THE COLLEGE WITH NO COURSES OR CREDITS / THE ELECTORAL COLLEGE
Page

128	"There was pandemonium": Jeffrey Toobin, *Too Close to Call: The Thirty-Six Day Battle to Decide the 2000 Election* (New York: Random House, 2002), p. 18
128	"We got…really close": ibid.
128	"our seven-minute presidency": ibid.
129	"I have…its wisdom": Thomas Jefferson letter to Edmund Pendleton, August 26, 1776, in Jean M. Yarbrough, editor, *The Essential Jefferson* (Indianapolis/Cambridge: Hackett Publishing Company, Inc., 2006), p. 141
134	"a corrupt bargain": Daniel Feller, "Campaigns and Elections: The Campaign and Election of 1824," Miller Center. *www.millercenter.org/president/jackson/campaigns-and-elections*
139	"It's time…our president": Jonathan Mahler and Steve Eder, "The Electoral College is Hated by Many. So Why Does It Endure?" *New York Times*, November 10, 2016. *www.nytimes.com/2016/11/11/us/politics/the-electoral-college-is-hated-by-many-so-why-does-it-endure.html*
139	"The Electoral…a democracy": ibid.
143	"we may…Presidential election": *Bush v. Gore*, 531 U.S. 98 (2000)

CHAPTER 13: PARDON ME? / PRESIDENTIAL PARDONS
Page

146	"I am not a crook": "Nixon Tells Editors, 'I'm Not a Crook.'" Carroll Kilpatrick, *Washington Post*, November 18, 1973. *www.washingtonpost.com/politics/nixon-tells-editors-im-not-a-crook/2012/06/04/gJQA1RK6IV_story.html?utm_term=.515bb0f1b9f0*
146	"suffered enough": "Ford Gives Pardon to Nixon, Who Regrets 'My Mistakes'," Hon Herbers, *New York Times*, September 9, 1974. *https://archive.nytimes.com/www.nytimes.com/learning/general/onthisday/big/0908.html#article*
146	"full, free…have committed": Presidential Proclamation 4311 of September 8, 1974 by President Gerald R. Ford granting a pardon to Richard M. Nixon. *https://catalog.archives.gov/id/299996*
148	"the mercy of government": Federalist No. 74
148	"restore the…the commonwealth": Federalist No. 74
148	"The traitors…be impoverished": Michael Ross, "President Andrew Johnson's Pardons of Former Confederates," C-SPAN, MARCH 11, 2015. *www.c-span.org/video/?c4691942/president-andrew-johnsons-pardons-confederates*
148	"fully restore…whole people": "Andrew Johnson, Proclamation 179—Granting Full Pardon and Amnesty for the Offense of Treason Against the United States During the Late Civil War," December 25, 1868, American Presidency Project. *www.presidency.ucsb.edu/documents/proclamation-179-granting-full-pardon-and-amnesty-for-the-offense-treason-against-the*

149   "to heal our country": Lee Lescaze, "President Pardons Viet Draft Evaders," *Washington Post,* January 22, 1977. *www.washingtonpost.com/archive/politics/1977/01/22/president-pardons-viet-draft-evaders/dfa064a5-83fc-4efb-a904-d72b390a909e/?utm_term=.7b9253a22685*

150   "those who...second chance": Peter Baker, "Alice Marie Johnson Is Granted Clemency by Trump After Push by Kim Kardashian West," *New York Times,* June 6, 2018. *www.nytimes.com/2018/06/06/us/politics/trump-alice-johnson-sentence-commuted-kim-kardashian-west.html*

150   "did not...avoid sentence": *United States v Wilson*, 32 U.S. 7 Pet.150. *www.supreme.justia.com/cases/federal/us/32/150/case.html*

151   "no person...own case": Nina Totenberg, "Could Trump Pardon Himself? Probably Not" National Public Radio, July 29, 2017. *ww.npr.org/2017/07/29/539856280/could-trump-pardon-himself-probably-not*

153   "for the sake...kindness": Stuart Winer, "President, Justice Minister Unveil Eased Pardons Plan for Israel's 70th Birthday, *Times of Israel*, March 26, 2018. *www.timesofisrael.com/president-justice-minister-unveil-eased-pardons-plan-for-israels-70th-birthday/amp*

153   "Our long...is over": Gerald Ford, "Remarks on Taking the Oath of Office," August 9, 1974, American Presidency Project. *www.presidency.ucsb.edu/documents/remarks-taking-the-oath-office*

CHAPTER 14: "YOU'RE HIRED! (MAYBE.) YOU'RE FIRED!" / THE UNITARY EXECUTIVE
Page

154   "Breaking news...from office": Michael D. Shear and Matt Apuzzo, "F.B.I. Director James Comey Is Fired by Trump," *New York Times,* May 9, 2017. *www.nytimes.com/2017/05/09/us/politics/james-comey-fired-fbi.html?login=smartlock&auth=login-smartlock*

155   "a made-up story": Philip Bump, "Timeline: What We Know about Trump's Decision to Fire Comey," *Washington Post,* January 15, 2018. *www.washingtonpost.com/news/politics/wp/2018/01/05/timeline-what-we-know-about-trumps-decision-to-fire-comey/?utm_term=.72b409cccf52*

155   "You are...the Bureau": ibid.

155   "nutjob": ibid.

156   "personally allied to him": Federalist No. 76

156   "independent and public-spirited men": Federalist No. 76

157   "I have...the executive." "How President Washington Made the First Appointments," George Washington's Mount Vernon. *www.mountvernon.org/george-washington/the-first-president/how-president-washington-made-the-first-appointments*

157   "removable from...United States": Raphael, *Mr. President,* p. 161

157   "violent...the Government": Raphael, *Mr. President,* p. 161

157   "no explanation...any President" Fergus M. Bordewich, *The First Congress: How James Madison, George Washington, and a Group of Extraordinary Men Invented the Government* (New York: Simon & Schuster, 2016), p. 135

157   "great want of temper" Bordewich, p. 133

157   "the instances...United States": Raphael, *Mr. President,* p. 162

158   "the future...of America": Raphael, *Mr. President,* p. 164

160   "I'm the…is best": "Bush: 'I'm the decider' on Rumsfeld," CNN, April 18, 2006. *www.cnn. com/2006/POLITICS/04/18/rumsfeld*

CHAPTER 15: IS ANYBODY THERE? / CONTINUITY IN GOVERNMENT
Page

164   "I'm on…the authorities": History Commons, "Complete 911 Timeline." *www.historycommons. org/project.jsp?project=911_project*

165   "Evacuate the…the building": "Interview with Jim Matheson, Logan, Utah, November 19, 2001." *www.loc.gov/item/afc911000162*

165   "Oh my…suicide mission": History Commons, ibid.

169   "Natural epidemics…of all": Ben Farmer, "Bioterrorism Could Kill More People Than Nuclear War, Bill Gates to Warn World Leaders," *Telegraph*, February 18, 2017. *www.telegraph. co.uk/news/2017/02/17/biological-terrorism-could-kill-people-nuclear-attacks-bill*

CHAPTER 16: THE PRESIDENT AND VICE PRESIDENT HAVE LEFT THE BUILDING / PRESIDENTIAL SUCCESSION
Page

176   "Get him…of here": Howell Raines, "Reagan Wounded in Chest by Gunman; Outlook 'Good' after 2-Hour Surgery; Aide and 2 Guards Shot; Suspect Held," *New York Times*, March 30, 1981. *archive.nytimes.com/www.nytimes.com/learning/general/onthisday/big/0330.html#article*

177   "Honey, I…the store": ibid.

177   "I am…White House": Richard V. Allen, "When Reagan Was Shot, Who Was 'in control' at the White House?" *Washington Post*, March 25, 2011. *www.washingtonpost.com/opinions/ when-reagan-was-shot-who-was-in-control-at-the-white-house/2011/03/23/AFJlrfYB_story. html?utm_term=.db8394dc4d3e*

178   "the men…to take": Brian C. Kalt, *Constitutional Cliffhangers: A Legal Guide for Presidents and Their Enemies* (New Haven: Yale University Press, 2012), p. 72

178   "the most…man contrived": Beeman, *Plain, Honest Men*, p. 305

180   "my intention…of government": Howard Schneider, "The Nuclear Winter White House," review of *Raven Rock*, by Garrett M. Graff, *Wall Street Journal*, May 6–7, 2017, p. C7. *www.wsj.com/ articles/the-nuclear-winter-white-house-1494006677*

180   "less informed…cable news": ibid.

183   "absent from…the duties": The Constitution of the Republic of South Africa. *www.gov.za/ DOCUMENTS/CONSTITUTION/constitution-republic-south-africa-1996-1*

CHAPTER 17: JANUARY 20TH. THE DUCK IS IN CHARGE. / INAUGURATION DAY
Page

186   "I have…Restore Hope": President George H. W. Bush, "Address to the Nation on the Situation in Somalia," December 4, 1992, American Presidency Project. *www.presidency.ucsb.edu/ documents/address-the-nation-the-situation-somalia*

186   "we will…armed gangs": ibid.

CHAPTER 18: AT WAR / EMERGENCY POWERS
Page

192   "He kept...of war": "Woodrow Wilson." *www.whitehouse.gov/1600/presidents/woodrowwilson*

192   "The world...for democracy": ibid.

193   "disloyal, profane...abusive language": Sedition Act of 1918, Section 3

193   "have always...declaring war": Eugene V. Debs, "The Canton, Ohio, Speech," June 16, 1918. *www.marxists.org/archive/debs/works/1918/canton.htm*

194   "Do not...of treason": ibid.

194   "it is...the world": ibid.

194   "continuous, active...our power": Peter Irons, *A People's History of the Supreme Court: The Men and Women Whose Cases and Decisions Have Shaped Our Constitution* (New York: Penguin Books, 2006), p. 274

194   "create[d] a...constitutional right": *Schenck v. U.S.*, 249 U.S. 47 (1919)

194   "When a...men fight": ibid.

195   "in certain...exceed power": Sanford Levinson, *Framed: America's 51 Constitutions and the Crisis of Governance* (Oxford: Oxford University Press, 2012), p. 355

195   "parchment barriers": Federalist No. 48

198   "In times...fall silent": "Inter Arma Enim Silent Leges Law and Legal Definition," USLegal. *https://definitions.uslegal.com/i/inter-arma-enim-silent-leges*

200   "I hated...was over": Irons, *A People's History*, p. 275

201   "I think...for acquittal": ibid.

201   "This man...my administration": James Chace, *1912: Wilson, Roosevelt, Taft and Debs—The Election that Changed the Country* (New York: Simon & Schuster, 2009), p. 275

201   "I have...you personally": ibid.

CHAPTER 19: AT WAR WITH BUGS / HABEAS CORPUS
Page

202   "national security priority": Jen Christensen and Debra Goldschmidt, "'Out of Control': How the World Reacted as Ebola Spread," CNN. *www.cnn.com/interactive/2014/11/health/ebola-outbreak-timeline*

204   "I feel...Constitutionally just": Jason Hanna and Ashley Fantz, "Maine Nurse Won't Submit to Ebola Quarantine, Lawyer Says," October 29, 2014. CNN. *www.cnn.com/2014/10/29/health/us-ebola*

204   "I remain...my freedom": ibid.

204   "The conditions...her liberty" ibid.

205   "confinement of...or forgotten": William Blackstone, *Commentaries on the Laws of England, Volume 1*, p. 98

205   "fatal evil": Federalist No. 84

205   "Rebellion or invasion": Kurland and Lerner, editors, *The Founders' Constitution, Volume 3.* *http://press-pubs.uchicago.edu/founders/documents/a1_9_2s8.html*

206   "most respectfully...an end": R. B. Taney, ex parte Merryman, 17 Federal Cases 144 (1861)

207   "the Constitution...the power": James A. Dueholm, "Lincoln's Suspension of the Writ of Habeas Corpus: An Historical and Constitutional Analysis," *Journal of the Abraham Lincoln Association*, Volume 29, Issue 2, Summer 2008, pp. 47–66. *http://hdl.handle.net/2027/spo.2629860.0029.205*

207   "a power…the Constitution": R. B. Taney, ex parte Merryman

207   "the people…of laws": R. B. Taney, ex parte Merryman

208   "apprehension, detention…communicable diseases": United States Code Annotated, Title 42. The Public Health and Welfare, Chapter 6A—Public Health Service, Subchapter II—General Powers and Duties, Part G—Quarantine and Inspection. Section 264 (b). *www.govinfo.gov/content/pkg/USCODE-2011-title42/html/USCODE-2011-title42-chap6A-subchapII-partG-sec264.htm*

209   "Commandeer or…the emergency": U.S. Centers for Disease Control and Prevention, "Public Health Emergency Law," Unit 4. *www.cdc.gov/phlp/docs/PHEL_3_1_UNIT_3_June_10_2009.pdf*

209   "an unprecedented…American people": Phyllis Schlafly, "Where Do Politicians Go In Their Afterlife?" Eagle Forum, December 19, 2001. *www.eagleforum.org/column/2001/dec01/01-12-19.shtml*

209   "governors into dictators": Association of American Physicians and Surgeons, Inc., "AAPS Analysis: Model Emergency Health Powers Act (MEHPA) Turns Governors into Dictators," December 3, 2001. *www.aapsonline.org/testimony/emerpower.htm*

210   "The governor…repel invasion": Constitution of the State of Florida

210   "war, invasion…public emergency": Constitution of the Republic of South Africa

211   "(a) the life…and order": ibid.

211   "action taken…a declaration": ibid.

211   "The court…entirely rational": Robert Bukaty, "Judge Rejects Attempt to Isolate Nurse," *Associated Press*, October 31, 2014. *www.apnews.com/80060d5318a5480f8bd8bef6a2c0bb00*

212   "a good…and gratitude": ibid.

212   "I don't trust her": Julia Bayly and Jackie Farwell, "After Kaci Hickox Wins Court Reprieve, Lepage Says He Doesn't Trust Her," *Bangor Daily News*, October 31, 2014. *www.bangordailynews.com/2014/10/31/news/aroostook/judge-requires-monitoring-wont-ban-kaci-hickox-from-public-places-on-ebola-fears*

CHAPTER 20: WE CAN CHANGE IT, RIGHT? / AMENDING THE CONSTITUTION
Page

213   "Equality of…of sex": Equal Rights Amendment. *https://catalog.archives.gov/id/7452156*

214   "A woman…and mother": "The Equal Rights Amendment Falters, and Phyllis Schlafly Is the Velvet Fist Behind the Slowdown," *People*, April 4, 1975. *www.people.com/archive/the-equal-rights-amendment-falters-and-phyllis-schlafly-is-the-velvet-fist-behind-the-slowdown-vol-3-no-16*

214   "Preserve us…ERA sham": Rosalind Rosenberg, *Divided Lives: American Women in the Twentieth Century* (New York: Macmillan, 1992), p. 225

216   "This constitution…become necessary": Kurland and Lerner, editors, *The Founders' Constitution, Volume 2*. *http://press-pubs.uchicago.edu/founders/documents/preambles8.html*

217   "evil": Federalist No. 62

218   "would eat…the amendment": John Heltman, "27th Amendment or Bust," *American Prospect*, May 30, 2012. *www.prospect.org/article/27th-amendment-or-bust*

221   "clogged": Kurland and Lerner, editors, *The Founders' Constitution, Volume 2*. *http://press-pubs.uchicago.edu/founders/documents/preambles7.html*

223   "The ERA...and constitutionally": Helen Andrews, "Where Are the Socially Conservative Women in This Fight?," New York Times, April 27, 2019. *www.nytimes.com/2019/04/27/opinion/sunday/conservative-women.html*

CHAPTER 21: GRADING THE CONSTITUTION
Page

224   "reflection and choice": Federalist No. 1

225   "I would...year 2012": Joshua Keating, "Why Does Ruth Bader Ginsburg Like the South African Constitution So Much?" *Foreign Policy*, February 6, 2012. *www.foreignpolicy.com/2012/02/06/why-does-ruth-bader-ginsburg-like-the-south-african-constitution-so-much*

225   "We are...perfect union": ibid.

225   "Is it...United States": Jeff Jacoby, "Ganging up on Ginsburg—Way Too Quickly," *Boston Globe*, February 8, 2012. *www.bostonglobe.com/opinion/2012/02/08/ganging-ginsburg-way-too-quickly/JQ5H08NIS4l4UTLvJlwbrI/story.html?s_campaign=8315*

227   "For God... her Independence": Derek Hawkins, "In a First, Texas Boys State Votes to Secede from Union," *Washington Post,* June 26, 2017. *www.washingtonpost.com/news/morning-mix/wp/2017/06/26/in-a-first-texas-boys-state-votes-to-secede-from-the-union/?utm_term=.c0a2c6e733d7*

CHAPTER 22: NOW WHAT?
Page

234   "it is...and perpetuate": Federalist No. 14

BIBLIOGRAPHY

There are many books for young readers about the US Constitution. We do not cite them here, partly because they are so numerous and partly because they supply a more traditional and comprehensive overview of the Constitution than our book does. In researching the Constitutional Convention of 1787 and the Framers' decisions that affect Americans today, we consulted a wide range of online, print, primary, and secondary sources, as you can see in the Notes. The following books were especially helpful.

SELECTED BOOKS

Amar, Akhil Reed. *American's Constitution: A Biography.* New York: Random House, 2005.

Beeman, Richard. *Plain, Honest Men: The Making of the American Constitution.* New York: Random House, 2009.

Bickerstaff, Steve. *Lines in the Sand: Congressional Redistricting in Texas and the Downfall of Tom DeLay.* Austin: University of Texas Press, 2007.

Epps, Garrett. *American Epic: Reading the U.S. Constitution.* Oxford: Oxford University Press, 2013

Hakim, Joy. *The History of US: From Colonies to Country: 1735–1791.* New York: Oxford University Press, 2007.
    The History of US: The New Nation: 1789–1850. New York: Oxford University Press, 2007.

King, Anthony. *The Founding Fathers v. The People: Paradoxes of American Democracy.* Cambridge: Harvard University Press, 2012.

Klarman, Michael. *The Framers' Coup: The Making of the United States Constitution.* New York: Oxford University Press, 2016.

Klarman, Michael. *The Framers' Coup: The Making of the United States Constitution.* New York: Oxford University Press, 2016.

Kurland, Philip B. and Ralph Lerner (eds). *The Founders' Constitution.* *http://press-pubs.uchicago.edu/founders/tocs/toc.html.*

Levinson, Sanford. *Framed: America's 51 Constitutions and the Crisis of Governance.* Oxford: Oxford University Press, 2012.

Our Undemocratic Constitution: Where the Constitution Goes Wrong (And How We the People Can Correct It). Oxford: Oxford University Press, 2006.

McGann, Anthony J., Charles Anthony Smith, Michael Latner, Alex Keena. *Gerrymandering in America: The House of Representatives, the Supreme Court, and the Future of Popular Sovereignty.* Cambridge: Cambridge University Press, 2016.

Paulsen, Michael Stokes and Luke Paulsen. *The Constitution: An Introduction.* New York: Basic Books, 2015.

Rakove, Jack N. *Original Meanings: Politics and Ideas in the Making of the Constitution.* New York: Alfred A. Knopf, 1996.

The Annotated U.S. Constitution and Declaration of Independence. Cambridge: The Belknap Press of Harvard University Press, 2009.

ARTICLES AND AMENDMENTS
CITED IN FAULT LINES IN THE CONSITITUTION

INDEX

democracy 91, 226; and
election process, 26; and
eligibility for office, 110,
116; and habeas corpus, 205;
and inauguration, 189; and
pardon, 152; and secession,
92, 226; and succession,
190; and unitary executive,
161; and voting districts, 77
Brookings Institution, 183
Burnett, Deena, 164–165
Burnett, Tom, 164–165, 168
Burr, Aaron, 132–133
Bush, George H. W., 127; and
inauguration, 185–186, 188;
and pardon, 150–151, and
succession, 177, 184; and
veto, 51
Bush, George, W., 155; and
continuity in government,
174; and Electoral College,
127–128, 141, 142–143; and
succession, 180; and Senate,
33, 35; and veto, 46–48; and
unitary executive, 160
Butler, Pierce, 49
Butterfield, Alexander, 145

C
cabinet, 28, 89, 115, 189, 237,
238; and continuity in
government, 173; and
succession, 177–179,
182–184; and the unitary
executive, 157, 159–161
California, 199; and
congressional districts,
76, 77; and continuity
in government, 174; and
direct democracy, 90; and
Electoral College, 135,
136, 142; and eligibility for
office, 109, 115–116; and
pardon, 152; and secession,

229; and Senate, 35, 41, 45;
and succession, 182; and
unitary executive, 161
Canada, 18; and pardon, 152–
153; and voting districts, 77;
and voting rights, 102–103
capital, and Compromise of
1790, 81; and District
of Columbia, 80–85;
and location of, 81; and
other countries, 85; and
representation, 82–86; and
retrocession, 86
Carter, Jimmy, and capital,
82; and pardon, 149; and
succession, 180; and unitary
executive, 159
census, and congressional
districts, 64–66, 72,
74–75; and gerrymandering,
64–66, 72; and process, 64,
70, 72
Centers for Disease Control and
Prevention (CDC), 204,
208–209, 211–212
Cheney, Dick, 174, 180
CHIP, see State Children's
Health Insurance
Christie, Chris, 204
Churchill, Winston, 190
citizenship, 28–29, 54–56, 87,
198; and census, 72; and
District of Columbia, 80,
82–85, 86; and Electoral
College, 131; and eligibility
for office, 105–111, 113–117,
236
Civil Liberties Act, 199
civil rights, 51, 58
Civil War, 148, 227; and
eligibility for office, 108;
and habeas corpus, 206; and
voting rights, 95
Clay, Henry, 133–134

Cleveland, Grover, 136, 141
Clinton, Bill, 199; and
inauguration, 185–187, 188,
190; and pardon, 149; and
veto, 51
Clinton, Hillary Rodham, 154,
170; and Electoral College,
136, 139, 141
cloture, 57
Cold War, 174–175
Colombia, and habeas corpus,
211
Colorado, and filibuster, 60; and
terrorism funding, 35; and
voting districts, 76; and
voting rights, 102
Comey, James B., 154–155, 159
commander in chief, see
presidency
Commerce Clause, 208
Commission on Election
Integrity, 98
Committee for the Re-election
of the President (CREEP),
145
Compromise of 1790, and
capital, 81
Confederation Congress, 8, 19,
25
Congress, and amendment
process, 213–223, 236–237;
and bicameralism, 23–32;
and capital, 80–86; and
congressional districts,
64–79; and continuity in
government, 165–175; and
District of Columbia, 80–
86; and direct democracy,
91, 236; and Electoral
College, 128–131, 139–142,
235–236; and eligibility for
office, 104–111, 113–114;
and emergency powers,
192–199; and Equal Rights

Photo credit Sam Bond

CYNTHIA LEVINSON writes award-winning nonfiction books about social justice for young readers, including *We've Got a Job: The 1963 Birmingham Children's March; The Youngest Marcher: The Story of Audrey Faye Hendricks, a Young Civil Rights Activist;* and *Watch Out for Flying Kids: How Two Circuses, Two Countries, and Nine Kids Confront Conflict and Build Community.* She also braids bread with six strands, juggles up to two balls, and takes a constitutional most days.

You can learn more about Cynthia and her books at *www.cynthialevinson.com.*

SANFORD (SANDY) LEVINSON has taught in both the Law School and the Department of Government at the University of Texas for almost forty years and is a regular visiting professor at the Harvard Law School. He is the author of several books for adults on the Constitution and writes frequently for a variety of newspapers, magazines, and blogs. In addition, he is interested in public monuments and symbols; he has an extensive collection of prints, photographs, and objects (such as cereal boxes) that depict the American flag in one way or another. He is also a huge fan of sea otters.

The co-authors have four thoroughly splendid grandchildren and divide their time between Austin, Texas, and Boston, Massachusetts.